THE
FASHION
YEAR

THE FASHION YEAR

GENERAL EDITOR · BRENDA POLAN

ZB

ZOMBA BOOKS

FIRST PUBLISHED IN GREAT BRITAIN IN 1983
BY ZOMBA BOOKS, ZOMBA HOUSE,
165-167 WILLESDEN HIGH ROAD, LONDON, NW10 2SG

© Zomba Books

ISBN 0 946391 02 5 (paperback)

ISBN 0 946391 03 3 (hardcover)

Typeset by Keyline Graphics, London

Printed by Toppan Printing Co (S) Pte Ltd, Singapore

Designed by John Gordon

Production Services by Book Production Consultants, Cambridge

First Edition

PHOTOGRAPHS BY:

Christopher Moore on pages 11, 14, 15, 18, 19, 22, 23, 26, 27, 30, 31, 33-41, 51, 54, 55, 58, 59, 61, 62, 63, 66, 67, 70, 71, 92, 93, 106, 107, 110, 111, 114, 115, 117, 118, 122, 123, 126, 127, 131-139, 141, 146, 150, 151, 156, 158, 159, 166-173, 186, 187, 189.

Frank Martin on pages 12-17, 20, 21, 24, 25, 28, 29, 52, 53, 68, 69, 72, 73, 76, 77, 80, 81, 108, 109, 142, 143, 149, 184, 188-191. (Courtesy Guardian Newspapers)

Nathalie Lamoral on pages 12, 13, 16, 44, 45, 48, 49, 105, 113, 116, 154.

Martin Argles on pages 85, 86, 87, 89, 120, 121, 124, 125, 155 (Courtesy Guardian Newspapers)

John Bishop on pages 42, 46, 47

Martin Brading on pages 74, 75

Yaki Halperin on pages 78, 79, 82, 83, 90, 91, 94, 95

Niall McInerney on pages 147, 148

Victor Yuan on pages 175, 178, 179, 183 (Courtesy of Express Newspapers)

Nick Briggs on page 176

Albert Watson on page 182 (Courtesy of Lancome)

Terence Donovan on page 183 (Courtesy of Express Newspapers)

Chris Grout-Smith on page 181 (Courtesy of Express Newspapers)

Guy-Yves Marineau on pages 160-165

Tim Graham (Sygma) on pages 98, 102

Press Association on pages 97, 100

Frank Spooner Pictures on page 99

Rex Features on page 99

Syndication International on pages 100, 101

London Express on page 103

COVER PHOTOGRAPHS BY:

Christopher Moore except Princess Diana by Rex Features

DRAWINGS BY:

Cilla Montague on page 81

Shari Peacock on pages 144, 145

Lynne Robinson on pages 87, 88

CONTENTS

INTRODUCTION

LADY, VAMP OR TRAMP?

● *By Brenda Polan*

There has never been a year in fashion when there was so little unity among the dictators of style and so much choice for its followers. Fashion historians currently in nappies are going to have an exceedingly hard time of it when they sit down to write an analysis of the period, but at least they will have the benefit of knowing what happened next.

The writers in this book do not have that advantage and thus, despite their experience and despite all the earnest debate which is, in 1983, animating the international fashion community, history may prove some of their judgements wrong. The advantage they do have is that they were there and they saw it happen and they were exposed, as the historian cannot be, to the political and economic climate, the fleeting cultural influences like a film or a youth cult, the intangible atmosphere of the times out of which the clothes were made.

Design in clothing changes faster than design in anything else except hairstyles and cosmetics. An architectural style must stand for a decade, a style in music or painting for a scarcely shorter period. A style in clothing can come and go in a month; it reflects the mood of that month and of no other. In the more formalised couture and high-price ready-to-wear reaches of the fashion world, a style lasts for half a year; it is modified, diluted, simplified and sold on the mass market where its influence may not be felt for six months or a year. Is it an accurate reflection of the moment it was first seen on the runways of Paris, Milan or New York or the moment the first young stylist paraded in a London club? Or is it an accurate reflection of the season when the mass market and the major part of the population felt right with it?

■ *Karl Lagerfeld*

One thing is clear: it is not, as the dedicated rubbishers of fashion would have it, all a matter of salesman's hype which exploits women's vanity and lack of judgement to make money. All human beings use clothing and decoration to define themselves and convey essential information to others, and as the human being and her/his preoccupations and moods change, so must the clothing. That men are largely excluded from this activity is a handicap, not proof of superiority.

One of the more important factors of fashion in 1983 was the emergence in Britain and in Japan of an almost androgynous style of dress which is permitting men more expression in their dress. Simultaneously, this style of dress questions all the status assumptions made by fashion ever since the first courtier tied an ermine tail to his hat.

Paris, the home and beating heart of status dressing, reacted to the joint assaults of Japan and the British designer, Vivienne Westwood, on its own sacred ground, by emphatically restating its belief in clothes which express wealth and clothes which express sexuality – markedly the sexual marketability of women.

Italy, too, turned its back on the shock of the new, reiterating its own brand of sporty, aggressive classicism based on luxurious fabrics and virtuoso skill in cut, colouring and accessorising. The United States, under the spell of a right-wing, Hollywood-bred administration, took a dive backwards towards a hard, glitzy glamour more in keeping with a wishful-thinking celluloid world than one of industrial recession, unemployment and a revived cold war. Even leisurewear carried implications of old-money pursuits and that relaxed modern-American style of dress dubbed designer sportswear took on fussy, formalised proportions and overdone detailing reminiscent of Paris couture and the rich men's playthings it dresses.

■ *Azzedine Alaia*

■ *Giorgio Armani*

It was not difficult to choose the four designers whose importance was crucial to fashion in 1983. The most brilliant exponent of the Parisian look at its most sexy and the man who sets the pace right at the top of the French fashion industry is German-born Karl Lagerfeld. In Paris, too, and heading the revival of overtly sexy dressing is the eccentric, till now obscure but, as far as other designers are concerned, influential Azzedine Alaia.

The man who made American-modern dressing possible and who, in his own country, continues to set the pace, rethinking and refining his line with an intellectual stamina almost unequalled is Giorgio Armani. And the designer who made possible the entire new Japanese movement in fashion, whose loyalty to the traditional Japanese method of permitting the fabric to be true to its own nature cleared the way for the rest, is Issey Miyake.

Even so, it is undoubtedly true that others, expert and non-expert, will feel they can put forward a better, entirely different roll of honour. That contentiousness, those violently expressed, passionately held opinions are part of what makes fashion, its wearing and its study, so compelling. The fashion shows in Paris and Milan are the best, the most exciting, the sexiest cabaret ever staged. They are the tip of the shiny, sun-refracting iceberg. An enormous industry, employer of millions, generator of fortunes, purveyor of magic and enchantment, hangs suspended beneath the waterline.

Clothing can be about nothing more than warmth and decency. It is rare, given a population living above starvation level, that that is all it is about. It is about self-expression, identity with a peer group, sensuality, imagination and power. It is also about individuality and a thousand exciting, challenging, outrageous or merely humorous ways of expressing it to the watching world. Here, more so than in any other human activity, you pays your money, you takes your choice. ●

■ *Issey Miyake*

PARIS

OPPOSITES ATTRACT

● *By Brenda Polan*

In one of those psychologists' free association word games, 'Paris' would still trigger the response, 'fashion', from most people. Whether the association would be made quite so rapidly the other way around is no longer so certain as it once was. Indeed, the army of women and men – the designers, their aides, assistants and hand-holders, their publicists, administrators, salespersons and crowd-controllers – who work so hard to maintain the city's role as world fashion leader, must occasionally heave a wistful sigh. Once it was so much easier. Once there were no challenges, no upstart Milanese asserting that Italian style beats French bravura, no impertinent New Yorkers hyping Seventh Avenue as fashion capital of the world.

Once, the simple phrase, 'a Paris gown', served to silence criticism and inspire imitation anywhere on the planet that laid claim to civilisation. Other people in other cities might make clothing; Paris made fashion.

True, the talent which flourished in Paris was rarely Paris-born and much was not even French-born. Among other foreigners, Worth was British, Balenciaga Spanish, Schiaparelli Italian, Lagerfeld is German and Kenzo Takada Japanese. But it was only in Paris that they could become stars, only there that their unique national characteristics and individual genius could shine as part of high fashion's mainstream. That this is still true today is an indication of the French fashion industry's single-minded determination to keep it so.

Where once it was complacent, it is now alert, outward-looking, flexible. Its complacency nearly cost it dear. So arrogant, introverted and careless had Paris haute couture become that is was not even watching when London, aided and abetted by the Swinging Sixties, crept up and stole its crown. Lost in its gilded elitist rituals, Paris had allowed itself to become irrelevant.

With one or two exceptions like André Courrèges and Emanuel Ungaro, Paris had ignored the social and economic changes which had been gathering pace since the war. Women's lives were changing and, consequently, what they wanted to wear was changing. Paris did not seem to notice any of this just as it did not seem to notice the shift of emphasis in women's self-image. Literature, music, the cinema had recast the heroine. No longer mature, sophisticated, passive, she was young, idealistic, aggressive instead. She wouldn't be seen dead in a Paris gown – unless it was by Courrèges, in shiny PVC and ended well above her child-like knees.

The Parisian establishment did not, of course, slump swooning on her little gilt chair for long. Beady, businesslike eyes narrowed, she gathered up her matronly skirts and staggered in pursuit of the thief and snatched back the bauble. Couturiers opened boutiques and started to design younger, fresher, cheaper ready-to-wear collections to complement and eventually to supplant their couture collections.

The Chambre Syndicale de la Couture Parisienne, the French co-ordinating co-operative organisation which looks after the interests of its member design houses in all kinds of areas – labour relations, the calendar of shows, design theft or 'copying', training, promotion and publicity – began to open its doors to more youthful talents. Rules on photography and embargoes on sketches were relaxed. The ready-to-wear collections, earlier and more theatrical than the couture showings, moved out of the marble, gilt and plush salons and into vast tents in Les Halles, the Bois de

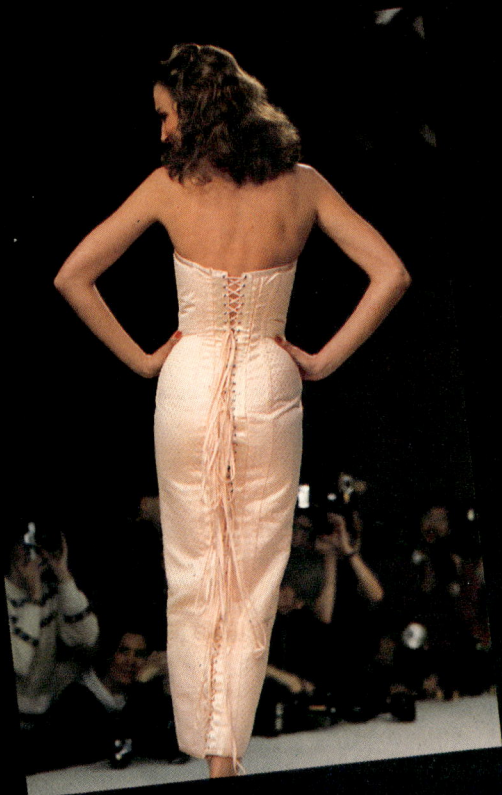

JEAN-PAUL GAULTIER

Boulogne, the Porte de Versailles or the Cour du Louvre. Here the loud music, the lack of oxygen, the crush and soaring temperatures, the theatrical lighting and ever more spectacular presentations of clothes that were more designers' sweeping statements than intelligent suggestions for a woman's wardrobe all contributed to a mood of near-hysteria which restored the smile to the face of the Paris fashion industry. There is nothing like it anywhere else in the world.

Last October's ready-to-wear showings of clothes for spring and summer 1983 were held in the Cour du Louvre, the venue which has so far found most favour with the several thousand international journalists and store and boutique buyers who throng to Paris twice a year. Other sites have called for long tube rides out to the suburbs or rain-sodden treks through the Bois.

The talk this time – and there is always plenty of talk, gossip, news, rumour, one-up-manship games: "My dear, you mean you missed so-and-so's show? Why it was the best this season..." – was not so much about the Paris look for spring or even Karl Lagerfeld's grand ball to launch his latest scent. It was mostly about the Japanese. Paris last October experienced what Figaro edgily joked was an invasion by the yellow peril: ten Japanese designers presenting their extraordinary collections as part of Prêt-à-Porter week.

Japanese designers are, of course, not new to Paris. Kenzo Takada arrived in 1970, the first to establish a base there and an almost immediate success, acquiring a cult-following among the well-heeled young. In the late seventies his were the shows that the fashion freaks (not press, not buyers, not even 'friends of the house', film stars or socialites, just fashion addicts

mainlining on the designer's bravura and self-generated hysteria) fought dirty to get into. Today they are more likely to be found lying, kicking and punching their way into a Claude Montana show or that of sleazy-minded enfant terrible, Jean-Paul Gaultier, whose circular stitched Lana Turner type bra tops for 1983 must surely owe something to Britain's Vivienne Westwood who did it all last season and has shown it all in Paris for two seasons.

In the 1980s Kenzo's shows are just as sensational as ever; it is just

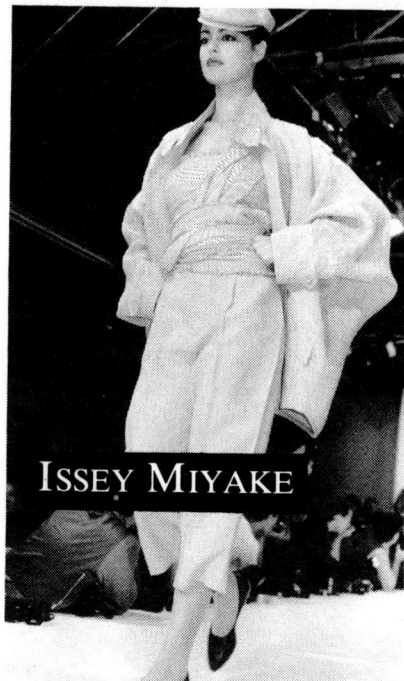

ISSEY MIYAKE

that, in the manner of most great fashion designers, he has settled into a style of dressing which is consistent and little changing from season to season. There are the tailored flannels and tweeds, youthful and, in their simplicity and leaning towards cross-overs and mandarin collars, reflecting an oriental influence. There are the bright, big-brush floral prints often made up into big, big smocks or mixed with smaller, neater florals or checks, stripes or plains. There are the big winter coats – huge

sheepskin or flapping tweed man's coat, the working man's caps, little boots and flat pumps, flouncy taffeta eveningwear, long and dramatic or naughtily short. His following, however, is as strong as ever and even justified, in 1982, the opening of the shop in London which devotes three floors to his clothes.

Issey Miyake and Kansai Yamamoto arrived in Paris not long after Kenzo but, although undeniably successful, did not take the city by storm in quite the same way. Yamamoto's work remained very Japanese in the manner of appliqué dragons on huge sweaters and jackets while Miyake became very much the designer's designer, admired by his peers and the fashion press for his almost miraculous sense of texture and volume, the fertility of his imagination and the ingenuity with which he constructed his intricate clothes – clothes which often, at the twitch of a model's shoulder, turned into another garment entirely. Press and buyers adored his shows, applauded till the rafters rang but did not, for the most part, quite see how these clothes would fit into the wardrobe of Mrs Average or even Lady Not-So-Average.

Which is rather the way they greeted the work of the New Japanese, some of which has a lot in common with Miyake's more self-indulgent productions. What is new and startling about the latest influx of Japanese designers is not their numbers so much as their Japaneseness. Although ethnic influences are obvious to a lesser or greater degree in the work of Miyake, Kansai and Kenzo, they all work very much in the tradition of European clothing.

The new Japanese work in their own ethnic tradition, concentrating on volume, abstract, bulky shapes

YOHJI YAMAMOTO

which have little to do with the shape of the body beneath, ingenious new textures – sometimes almost neurotically bizarre in concept – and absence of colour.

These clothes, which are more fully described in another chapter, made their first impact in Paris in March 1982 when Rei Kawakubo of Comme des Garcons and Yojhi Yamamoto showed for the first time outside the official calendar. Observers waited curiously for October to see what effect their instant acclaim would have on Paris's more established designers.

The answer seemed to be polarisation. Of the old-guard Japanese, Issey Miyake gravitated towards his compatriots, allowing a fuller rein to his instinct for abstract-shaped mass and rough, rich textures, while refusing to subscribe completely to what the Americans have labelled 'the beggarman look'. For this spring, as well as parachute pants with vertical draw-strings for arranging one leg shorter than the other and asymmetrical blobby sweaters, he has designed some covetably simple, if massy, clothes in rich earth tones and strong pastels.

But the rest of established Paris has moved as far away from the bruised and battered, torn and tattered beggarwoman as it is possible to recoil. There was, to their shows, a mood of traditional Paris chic and more than a little Paris ooh-la-la as models, used to striding along the runway in sporty culottes, full skirts and trousers, discovered how to wiggle along it in tight skirts and sheath dresses.

The Japanese are all clutter, bagginess and bulk; the home team went for a clean, lean outline, shortish more often than long, sharply tailored or curved to follow every one of the body's contours. Of course, there are relaxed, sporty

13

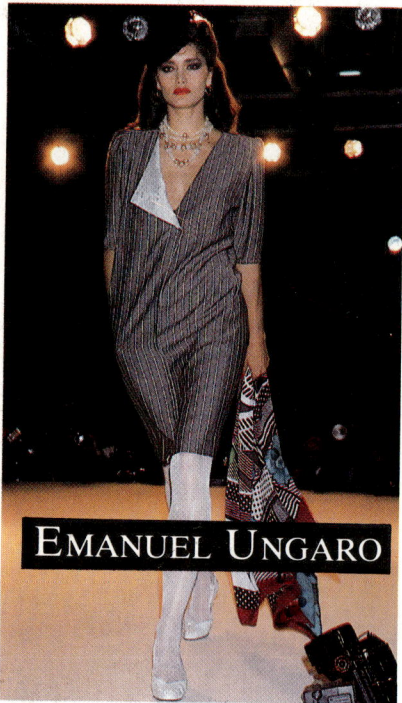

clothes for summer, particularly well done by Claude Montana whose themes are mostly from *Boys' Own:* the safari-jacketed explorer, the navy (officer class and jaunty matelot) and the military with epaulettes and Sam Browne belt.

But the strongest feeling is for the tippy-toe, gloved and hatted V-shaped woman, her shoulders slightly broadened, but far from square – more a shoulder-pad aided curve – emphatically belted at the waist or just below, pencil slender to the knee or mid-calf.

It is the shape which Karl Lagerfeld introduced at Chloé for autumn/winter 1982-3; then the waist was emphasised by breath-inhibiting patent leather corselet belts for which the fashion press, while conceding that they were sexy, saw little future. Women, in the last two decades, have become accustomed to being comfortably free of corsetry.

For spring Lagerfeld has developed the shape, sliding the corselet down over the hip bones in elasticated velvet and topping it

CLAUDE MONTANA

CLAUDE MONTANA

with another, narrower, leather belt at the natural waist. His pencil skirts button up the back and are left half undone to facilitate walking. His jacket is the freshest-looking in Paris or anywhere: a good easy shape with wide, curved shoulders, deep armholes and what he calls a 'hammer' sleeve. Beneath the one-button jacket goes what Lagerfeld calls his Schiller blouse: wide-collared and open to the waist in the manner of anguished, chest-baring romantic poets.

With this smart way of dressing go sophisticated accessories: ornate high-heeled shoes, elegant, wide-brimmed straw hats, ladylike gloves and the chunky plastic jewellery of the late fifties and early sixties – vulgar and jokey. Lagerfeld's jewellery for spring has a musical theme: piano keyboard belts and chokers, banjo brooches, music score belts and little trumpets and guitars dangling from the ears. His Arab-market be-sequinned evening wear revels in the same gaudy motifs while his cream lace, pearl-accessorised, Edwardian-looking evening dresses are all covetable tasteful restraint.

Chanel, the house for which Lagerfeld now designs the couture collection, fielded a new design team for its ready-to-wear collection, led by an ex-Lagerfeld assistant, Hervé Leger. He stuck faithfully to the 'little Chanel suit' in pastel tweed, in this case somewhat over-trimmed.

The late Coco Chanel herself was one of those designers who invented a way of dressing which worked spectacularly well for many women. Since her death a series of designers have marked time producing the same clothes and conceding shoulder pads here and a change of hemline there to fashion. Hervé Leger has not deviated, recreating the Chanel suits of the fifties. The

difference is that fashion has once more swung the way of the neat little, semi-tailored suit and that means applause for the house of Chanel.

Although Lagerfeld did not go to work at Chanel until January this year, his influence was observable in one or two outfits like the curve-shouldered, double-breasted navy jacket over crisp white pencil skirt and the see-through evening-wear.

Sonia Rykiel resembles Chanel in that her own style is stronger than any fashion movement. Her outline is long and lean; her fabric is chiefly soft, clinging wool or cotton jersey; her colour is mostly black. As far as she is concerned, this year the rest of Paris has decided to conform. She has two new skirts: a straight pencil shape to the knee which is softened two-thirds down by a flounce; and a long, hip–hugging version which

CHANEL

SONIA RYKIEL

THIERRY MUGLER

flares to mid-calf, slashed on one side to flash some leg.

Rykiel, perhaps in reaction to the Japanese smash-and-grab raid on her favourite colour, is much more colourful, exploring peachy pinks, periwinkle blue and some bright prints.

Thierry Mugler also consistently prefers a lean outline though, while Rykiel's is entirely her own and is almost liquid in the softness and discreet fluidity of its line and fabric, Mugler's is much more stylised. One feels that young Thierry spent summer weekend afternoons when he should have been out playing football, watching old movies on television with the curtains unhealthily drawn.

He has, whatever the reason, always had a passion for the 1940s and 50s. He loves glamour in its tawdry Hollywood version and it shows in the clothes he designs – a touch of Joan Crawford here, a soupçon of Marilyn Monroe there. His metallic alligator-print sheath dresses, short and long, were, without doubt, the sexiest clothes in Paris. Unfortunately, Mugler can rarely resist the temptation to outrageously gild the lily – so he slashed his beautiful dresses; little cuts, in places like the breast, the belly and the buttock, which gaped and caused worldly models to blush.

In addition, he designed some very classy suits with military details, some over-decorated banana republic dress whites, some stunning raglan-sleeved jersey sheath dresses (unslashed) and some wonderfully nostalgic sack dresses, back buttoning to a shoulder-blade revealed V. The first garments which he sent down the runway remain, however, the most memorable. They were big canvas coats in strong primary colours, with extravagantly curved shoulder-sleeve lines tapering in the

19

THIERRY MUGLER

YVES SAINT LAURENT

YVES SAINT LAURENT

body to stop at three-quarter length over pencil skirts in a strikingly modern interpretation of the massive-shouldered Mildred Pierce look he loves so much.

Yves Saint Laurent, the long-time darling of jet-set women with style, has also established a style based on outfits – like the trouser suit – which were gasp–making headline-hitters when he first introduced them but are now part of the basic vocabulary of every designer. He too opted for a trimmer line than recently, discarding the floating shawls and tunic shapes of recent collections in favour of neat, short jackets and neat, short skirts under straw boaters and razzy summer dresses in Carmen Miranda mood.

It was, decided a Paris feeling perhaps a trifle defensive, a spring and summer for upholding traditional femininity. For when the ordinary person playing our word association game, snaps back 'Fashion' in reply to: 'Paris' what she or he most probably has in mind is the lady on very high heels, all curves and dramatic hat, her be-gloved hand holding a long lead on the end of which lunges a French poodle.●

SPRING/SUMMER
MILAN

DOWNBEAT AND GROWNUP

● *By Brenda Polan*

J ust over a decade ago Italy's young designers made a move to throw off the country's old fashioned image as a source of heavy-handed couture for Roman matrons, nice knits and cheap, if stylish, shoes. Instead of showing their collection in the gilded salons of Rome or amid the renaissance splendours of Florence, they showed in Italy's industrial heartland, in Milan, the city whose name had already become synonymous with all that was exciting and fresh in industrial, interior and furniture design.

Their timing was excellent. The early seventies was a period of confusion in the fashion world. The influence of the London designers was waning and the new generation of Paris-based designers which still holds centre-stage today was just emerging. The Italians made their bid for pre-eminence with clothes more stylish than headline-grabbing, clothes which were much more wearable and timelessly smart than those produced anywhere else.

They used leather and suede in a way unthought of, reaching back to the renaissance for shapes, colours and a sense of richness which they applied not only to skins but to the silks that came from Como and the lush knitwear which the Missonis conjured from the memories of renaissance tapestries and dreams of medieval romance.

Once the Milan group was accepted as Italy's fashion vanguard, it began to equal Paris in importance and influence. Names like Armani and Versace took their place alongside those of Saint Laurent and Lagerfeld. The international buyers, the press and the rag-trade copyists divided their attention equally between the two great fashion capitals and although the last few years have seen serious challenges from the United States, Japan

LUCIANO SOPRANI

GIANNI VERSACE

and even (again) Britain, the dual pre-eminence continues.

But it has not been an easy or trouble-free or completely self-confident decade for either city. There are always divisions, jealousies, weaknesses when so many disparate designers try to work separately yet together. 'Milan' or 'Paris' must have a strong corporate identity to sell to the rest of the world, yet the several designers who make up 'Milan' and 'Paris' must maintain their own unique design identities.

Armani, for instance, is one of the most copied designers in the world. His signature is so strong that, quality aside, it is easy to copy. So last October, when Milan showed its clothes for spring and summer 1983, Armani chose, for the second season running, not to show his own-label collection on the runway but as a very Milanese still-life display backed up with a video. His feeling that the all-music, 50-girl, theatrical runway cabaret show is reaching the end of its days is probably correct. The expense, the strain, the wonderful opportunity such shows offer to copyists, and the terrible temptation to self-indulgence they offer to designers, all militate against them.

For it is when the Italian designers, justifiably celebrated for dressing women (and men) stylishly for all kinds of daytime activities, decide that the only true climax to a proper show is vampy cocktail dresses followed by uneasily grand evening wear, that they send you out disappointed. Similarly, since you cannot send a model out onto the runway but half-dressed, knitwear manufacturers like the Missonis are forced to make bottoms to go with their unequalled tops and they get a large percentage of them wrong thereby doing their merchandise an injustice since the

GIORGIO ARMANI FOR ERREUNO

MISSONI

GENNY

MARIUCCA MANDELLI FOR KRIZIA

eye focuses on the imperfection rather than the mouthwatering perfection above.

If Armani's point were taken and the grand opera of the runway show were abandoned, Italian style could be seen at its purest. Women would not be offered, as they were for last spring, Luciano Soprani's strange evening frocks: floating panels and swathes of vaguely Arabian, sort of African, slightly Caribbean, a bit Persian, marginally Indian furnishing fabrics. Nor would the Fendi sisters, advised by Karl Lagerfeld, feel compelled to go beyond the stunning statement of their fifties-style sheath dresses in black suede or heavy white cotton into the tacky regions of white chiffon bondage gear. And the brilliant Missonis would stop running up strange little skirts and shorts which look like the afterthoughts they were.

But once all this is discarded, Milanese style for spring and summer was a matter of clean and simple lines, a narrow V-shape, predominantly lean with shoulders slightly broadened but softly rounded in the manner favoured for several seasons by Mariucca Mandelli at Krizia, jackets and shirts gently bloused, the lower limbs clad in a pencil-straight skirt reaching to just beneath the knee, or relaxed trousers, some cropped but most full-length, often ending in a cuff. Mostly trousers were front-pleated or gathered and quite roomy in the leg; here and there the jeans-cut trouser made a return, tightly corsetting hips, bottom and thighs.

As always when clothes become simpler and more streamlined, accessories became more important last spring - in both senses of the word. Silly headdresses designed only for the runway were replaced by deliciously wearable broadrimmed straw hats, trilbys and

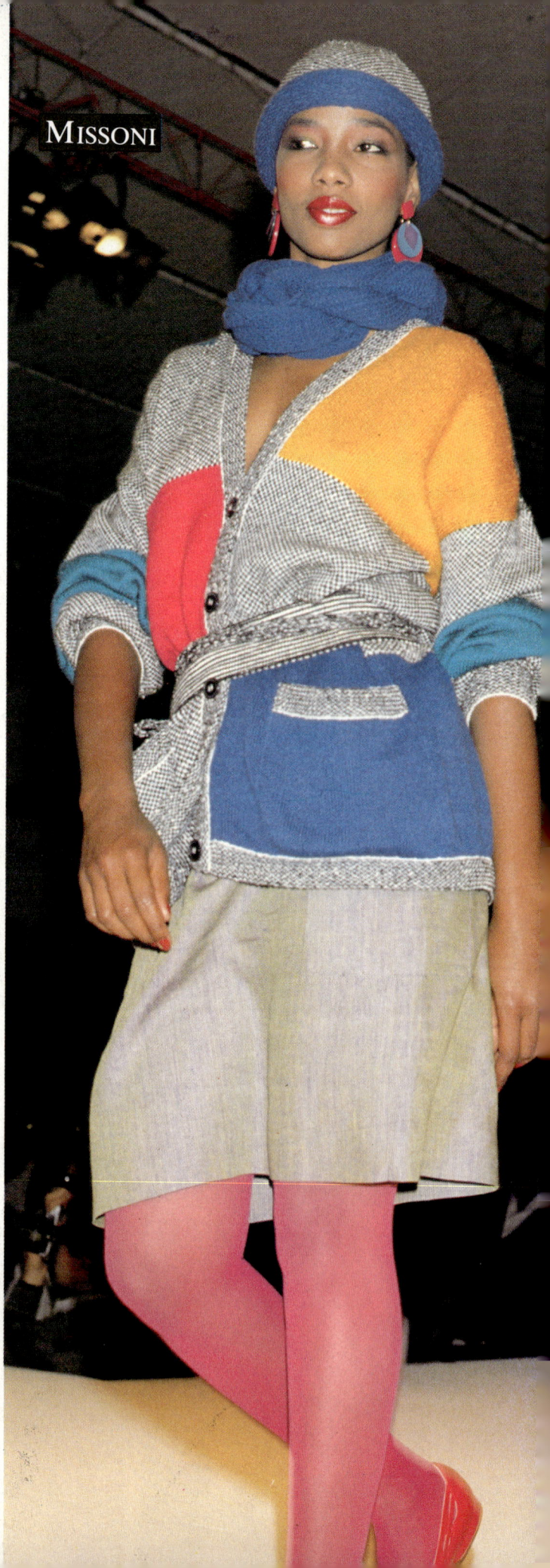

fedoras all meant to be sold and worn. Belts were less aggressive than previously but the Italians were telling women to wear two. Costume jewellery was abstract and strong with a fifties vulgarity to it and made in modern materials like shiny plastics, transparent Perspex, dull black metal or chrome.

Although Milan always offers good, imaginative and smart leisure wear, the prevailing mood was city-slick coloured in Milan's favourite shadow tones of black and white, grey, coffee, cream, some navy and white, some earthy, muddy or desert rock colours and the tobacco which Soprani always uses so well, often with black.

The sharp contrast of black and white worked most strongly on Armani's blouson-topped light-weight wool suits, on Gianni Versace's mixed checks and prints in glossy linen and on Luciano Soprani's Prince of Wales check trouser suits topped with a matching or plain duster coat. This is the Italian executive woman; at Fendi she even wore city grey pinstripe linen pants and a broad-shouldered

FENDI

SPORTMAX

28

CLAUDE MONTANA FOR COMPLICE

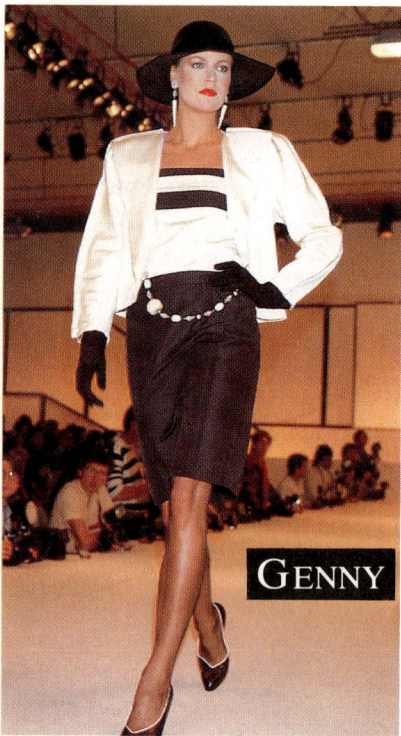

GENNY

jacket, her high-powered image reinforced by a crisp white cotton double-breasted waistcoat complete with important lapels. She dispenses, however, with a shirt and tie and the result was provocative in a witty way which is typically Italian. They do love menswear fabrics and shapes on women. For them, it seems to have an aggressively sexy appeal.

For Complice, Claude Montana again used the silver grey touched with white which always works well in this very sophisticated collection. His heavy cotton trouser suit, pants cropped just above the ankle, the jacket short and wide, demonstrated his ability, not always so clearly displayed in his own-label Parisian collection, to synthesise the sporty and the sharply chic.

The simpler outline brought with it a renaissance for the frock: a sensuous shift of silk at Armani; a soft, droopy cross-over dress, hip-belted and skirt-slashed at Gianfranco Ferre; dramatically curved shoulderline and slash-skirted to the hip at Krizia (in sea

MARIUCCA MANDELLI FOR KRIZIA

LAURA BIAGIOTTI

blue, green or cinnamon cotton); a narrow white linen shift with Mondrian-type inserts of vivid primary colour and a shirt-shaped hem at Laura Biagiotti.

Biagiotti's cashmeres represented the leanest line of all: sinuous tops and trousers in black, white and scarlet with dramatic three-cornered scarf-shaped panels looped around and tied at hip or waist. Mariucca Mandelli at Krizia showed a stronger, simpler, more graphic line: stylishly dramatic dark pencil-skirted suits with dashing white collars, lapels, wide bow ties and giant carnations. She also had some swingy jewel-coloured wool jackets and her animal of the season was an alligator who wrapped himself around intarsia sweaters, sometimes swallowing his own tail, and whose hide was embossed on cotton chintz and rubber to produce an extraordinary fabric which Mandelli used for cropped trousers and coats.

The pencil skirt was not unchallenged but it did look freshest, its length varying from above the knee all the way down in stages to just above the ankle. There were jaunty pleated skirts - prettiest were from Sportmax in cream linen with matching mandarin-collared jacket, reminiscent of the last days of the Raj and suitably topped with a straw topee, a look which was to gain popularity as the summer progressed. And there were some long, full skirts gathered into the waistband or a deep hip basque; as summer progressed these were to prove more successful than expected simply because they were more comfortable in hot weather than those flirty little cigarette skirts.

Anything peasanty looked decidedly wrong, however. Italy was in a city-slick mood, completely unrural and decidedly Milanese. ●

NEW YORK

A PERSONALITY CHANGE

● *By Jackie Moore*

The most surprising thing about the emergence of American fashion is that it has taken so long. As early as 1860 a census revealed a growing ready-to-wear industry in the United States and by the end of the century there was a thriving business making the kind of calico shirtwaister so eagerly snapped up today under the Ralph Lauren label. But this was virtually workwear. For fashion, the New World looked to the Old, once the home of those who sewed their life away in the sweatshops of lower East Side. To the workers and customers alike, fashion meant France.

There were a few false starts, usually concerned with another American phenomenon, the movies. Between the wars the influence of Adrian and Edith Head, through their film wardrobes for Garbo, Dietrich and Crawford affected women everywhere.

Yet this was still European fashion. Even when a talented young man called Mainbocher arrived on the New York scene in the 1930s he went to Paris to make his name, backed by a group of wealthy American women living in Europe. Ironically Mainbocher's clothes were frequently worn by Wallis Simpson. His backers must have held their breath at the thought of a possible future American Queen of England as their customer.

Even more ironic was the fact that when America finally got its own fashion First Lady, in the shape of Jackie Kennedy, she wore Paris couture or Seventh Avenue copies rather than original American design. For there was such a thing by then. .

It had taken an Englishman to give the Americans confidence in home-grown fashion. Charles James was born in Surrey in 1906, into a Cornish landowning, military family. Small wonder, perhaps, that his father never recovered from the shock of a dress designer as a son. He blamed some of it, possibly, on Harrow School, where the young Charles met such outré fellows as Cecil Beaton. His American mother proved more understanding.

During the 1930s James enjoyed his success, dressing such elegants as Gertrude Lawrence, travelling between London and Paris, and infuriating the French by selling dresses to be copied by American stores - an area till then reserved exclusively for the French.

At the outbreak of the Second World War he went to the United States. Despite regular bankruptcies, by the time he died in 1978 Charles James had helped establish the habit among American stores of buying American fashion. Still more important he had an influence on many young fashion students in the United States, an influence which is only just beginning to show.

The Charles James flavour that infiltrated many of the New York collections shown last October, was due to the retrospective exhibition of his work at the Brooklyn museum - an exhibition regarded by many locals as the work of America's greatest designer; they conveniently forget the Cornish connection.

The newly sophisticated mood of Spring '83 also owes something to two other recent exhibitions in the United States, those devoted to Balenciaga and his protegé, Hubert de Givenchy. The result was a new concentration on fit, on seams and darts, on well-groomed, grown-up clothes.

The biggest shock waves were felt at Calvin Klein. It had been Klein, with his easy-going separates, who had persuaded so much of the world that there was such a thing as American fashion.

His background is classic for the American designer of today. He was born into the Bronx

CALVIN KLEIN

KLEIN MOBBED BY MODELS

middle class Jewish community, and, he says: "Since the age of five, I've known that I wanted to design clothes and have my own business." He took himself and his sketches to the High School of Art and the Fashion Institute of Technology. His next logical step was into a coat and suit house on Seventh Avenue. Seventh Avenue is not just an address, it is the basis, the solid foundation, of American fashion. During the 1920s a group of investors, rather more far-sighted than even they imagined, built 498 and 550 Seventh Avenue, two

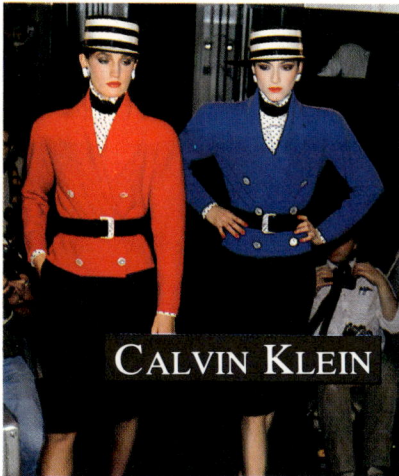

CALVIN KLEIN

monoliths into which they gathered the lower East Side manufacturers. Today many of the best names in New York fashion are still to be found in 550 and its environs.

Among the cluster of buildings on and around Seventh that house the success stories in American manufacturing are the young apprentice designers who will in turn become the leaders. Technical expertise in manufacture and immense skill in selling their wares made Seventh Avenue a formidable force, even in the days when copying Paris was the rule. This expertise helped the young Calvin Klein when, in 1968, he and a school friend Barry Schwartz produced their first collection of coats. Within five years he was successful enough to buy out his

former boss and move into his own premises just around the corner from Seventh Avenue. By then he had realised the growing importance of what the Americans call sportswear and Europe knows as elegant separates, the ideal clothes for the busy working woman. It was with these, relaxed and easy in silk, suede, cashmere, that Calvin Klein made his, and America's name.

All the more surprising, then, that his collection for Spring '83 was to prove so European in approach. Always aware of the body, and one of the first to see the importance of the exercise cult, his clothes are now ultra body-conscious. His aim, he said, was to "combine the refinement and elegance of the couture tradition with my belief that clothes should be realistic and wearable". The result was crisp satin gabardine jackets fitted into and cropped at the waist, with sharp revers and mother-of-pearl double-breasted fastenings

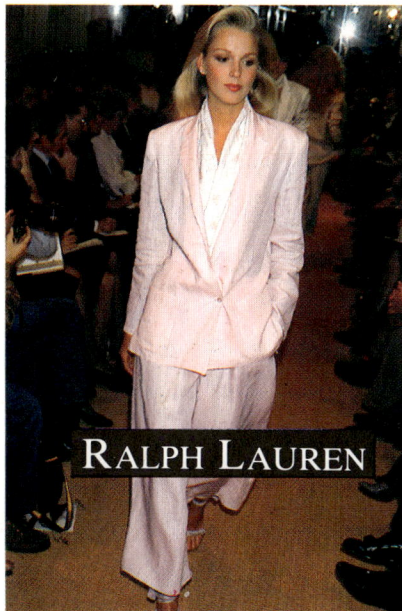

RALPH LAUREN

over straight flannel trousers or short slim skirts, with high collared blouses, black cravats and fob watches tucked into the jacket pockets. Or little peplum tops in spotted crêpe de Chine, the sleeves cut full at the shoulder and

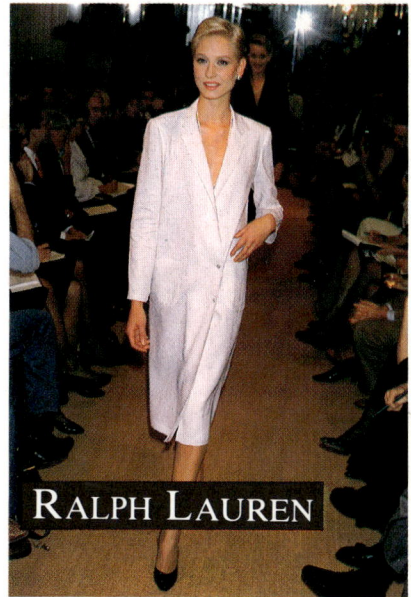

RALPH LAUREN

narrowing to the wrist, over tight crêpe skirts buttoning down the side.

Sexy bustier tops in white piqué had cuffs turned over to show the black lining, and were again worn with narrow little sidebuttoned skirts. The peplum suits were repeated in camelia-printed black and ivory silk crêpe de Chine.

Evening dresses were slinky wraps of fuschia or ivory satin crêpe with Mildred Pierce shoulders or they were strapless peplums of diamanté stripes over slim black satin skirts. Klein says that the collection was dedicated to the memory of Vogue magazine's Baron Nicky de Gunsberg who died two years ago. "He," says Klein, "always encouraged me to take things one step further." This move to ultra-sophistication proved too much for Calvin's European customers and admirers (a weakening pound and a strengthening dollar caused the closure of his London shop in late 1982), but the Americans loved the glamour.

The second fork of the two-pronged attack made by New York on international fashion came from another New Yorker, Ralph Lauren. He arrived on the design

PERRY ELLIS

DONNA KARAN AND LOUIS DELL 'OLIO FOR ANNE KLEIN

OSCAR DE LA RENTA

GEOFFREY BEENE

BILL BLASS

HALSTON

scene by another, quite valid route. Lauren was a menswear buyer, like his Italian counterpart, Giorgio Armani.

It was Lauren who put the world into fringed suedes, cowboy boots, Prairie skirts and frilled denim skirts. Last winter he perfected the Early American Pioneer as well as Indian reservation chic. For spring he too had some shocks up his sleeve. Not for him the European way. On the contrary, he edited his collection down as far as anyone dared. His day clothes were all in black, white or palest blue and pink printed linen. As Klein's silhouette became restricted, Lauren's loosened. His blazers were oversized, his trousers easy, tops were full artist's smocks, dresses soft, fluid and calf length with just a touch of silk cord at the waist. Later in the day there were heavier linens, again in black or white, with halter-necked dresses under narrow blazers. There was a summer version of his winter winner, a coat dress with low double-breasted fastening, in white linen.

Summer evenings called for his favourite tuxedo suits or slim, relaxed trousers or tunic suits with a little diamanté embroidery on pockets or neckline. This is the kind of easy elegant fashion that we have grown accustomed to as American style, which is no doubt why it was greeted with much relief by European buyers.

Five years ago another ex-buyer set up his own shop, with the avowed intent of bringing fun to fashion. Perry Ellis does not appear to have the usual background for fashion. He comes from the South, from Portsmouth, Virginia, one of the more conservative parts of the United States. Perhaps this was why, at first, his interest in colour and fabrics was channelled towards a business career, albeit in retailing.

He took his B.A. and later his M.A. degrees in business and retailing and found his first job as a buyer for a department store in Richmond, Virginia. His interest in styling led him in 1968 to a job as design director for a New York manufacturer and ten years later he was head of his own company. In just a few years he has won all the awards there are and has become the darling of the younger fashion set.

Like any fashion innovator he sometime shocks, but hopes, he says, "to amuse". His spring collection had a Spanish flavour, with matador boleros and full, sometimes ankle length skirts, but his major story centred on the waist. There were belts, at least 20cms deep, with large silvery buckles. There were deep waistbands on dirndl skirts and extra-wide trousers. And there were imitation belts knitted into sweaters. Ellis has always been strong on sweaters and produces his own 'knit it yourself' packs. For spring he liked trompe l'oeil jokes, like the fake jewelry knitted into his little jerseys, or the butterflies, and, particularly, the flesh-coloured insets on black sweaters giving the effect of an off-the-shoulder or strapless top.

Sportswear was not exclusively the preserve of Calvin Klein. A label steadily growing in importance is that of Anne Klein. The owner of the name, who made her fame in the 1960s with imaginative separates, died some years ago. Her successor was a young designer called Donna Karan, who had worked with Anne Klein for several years. She, and an old fashion school friend Louis Dell'Olio, now design everything from cashmeres to furs. Quietly, with a minimum of fuss, they have been perfecting Anne Klein's own art, of producing good-looking separates that will come together to provide clothes to wear throughout

the day and evening. The result is, somehow, particularly good New York style, relaxed but chic, pared down yet effective. Using mainly ivory, ebony and topaz, in cashmere, crêpe de Chine, gabardine and jersey the spring silhouette was long and slim, defining the waist at times but still easy to wear, using the colours in blocks to emphasise the lean shape.

The return of European-style sophistication to the New York scene has brought attention back to the established designers. If fashion is going to be grown-up and slick, then these are the men who will show everyone how to do it.

Oscar de la Renta learned his techniques from European masters and, if fashion dictates a fitted wool jacket with a sleek skirt, he can cut it better than most. His peplum suits are in white cotton piqué, with a crisp polka dot silk blouse, and the de la Renta signature, a Pussy cat bow at the neck. The couture based designers all share a liking for lace, used to overlay a hem, or trim a yoke, and de la Renta's demure, calf length creamy silk dresses had neat satin belts and ecru lace at hem and square-yoked top.

In 1942 the cosmetic house of Coty introduced a fashion award, to encourage and promote American fashion. Geoffrey Beene has won eight Coty awards to date, the most ever given to one designer. If his parents had had their way he would have taken quite another path. Geoffrey, another Southern son, from Haynesville, Louisiana, should have been a doctor but he spent his time at lectures sketching the Adrian dresses he had seen in films. Not surprisingly, he failed his exams and was sent to the University of California to try again. Geoffrey never made the course, because he was waylaid by the chance of a job as assistant in the display department

OSCAR DE LA RENTA

GLORIA SACHS

of California's famous store, I. Magnin.

Once he had taken the first step into the fashion business he decided he would do the job properly. He went to Paris for intensive training in designing, sewing and cutting, learning this last art from the British master of the bias cut, Molyneux. Back in New York he worked with several companies, then, in 1963, unveiled his first collection under his own name. A shy, somewhat reticent man, Beene and his original partner still own the company and Beene likes it that way. As his Rolls Royce shows, he does well enough as it is, with his own perfume and licencing arrangements for everything from tights and sun glasses to household linens. His spring '83 collection was regarded as among the best in New York, filled with superb little couture touches, like the hand-rolled fluted collars, delicate tucking, and the Art Deco

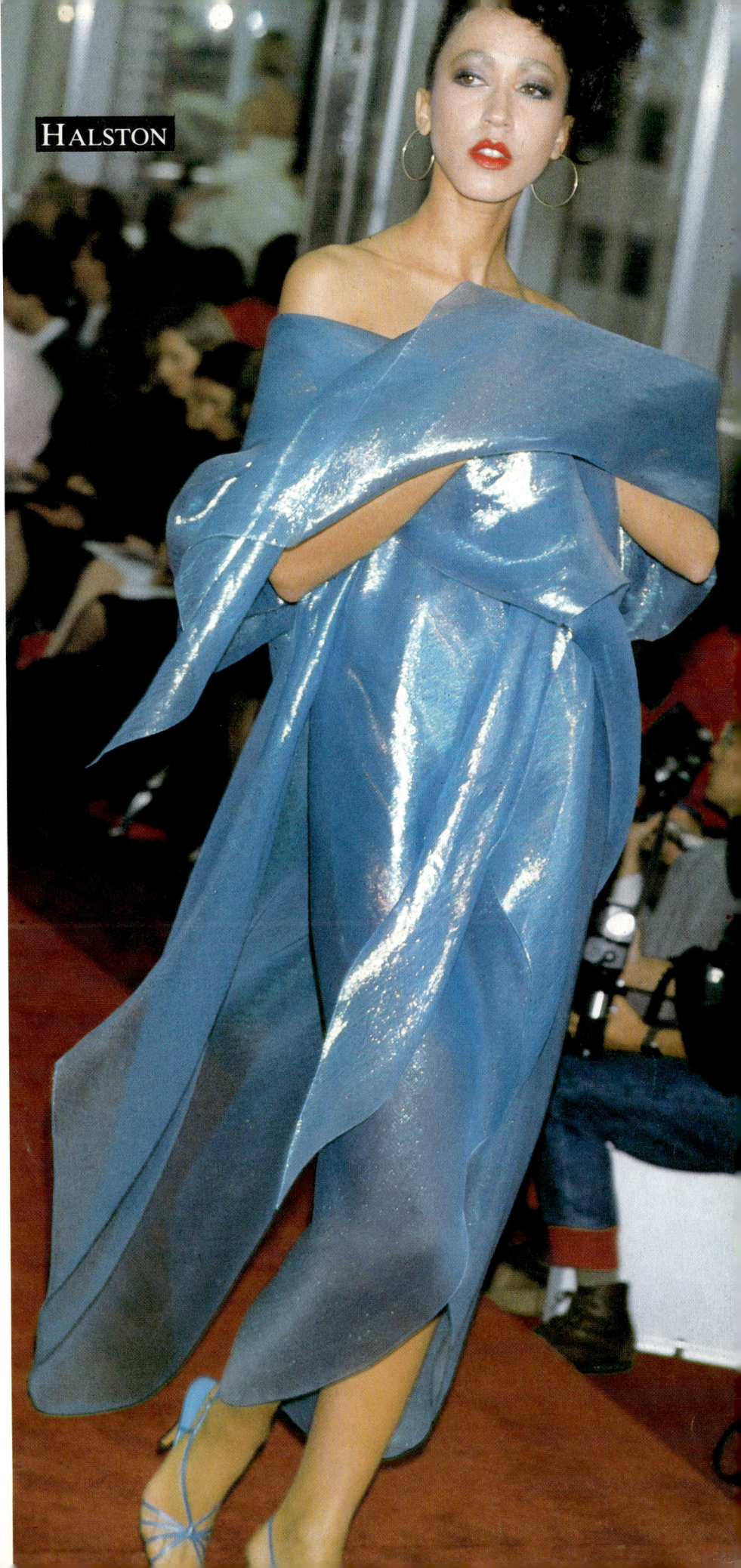

stitching on the sapphire bands on a grey silk satin dress with low hip sash and dropped shoulders. Like de la Renta he added bands of lace to his hems, starched and Paisley patterned on silk organza.

Bill Blass makes up the couture triumvirate. He too is Paris couture-minded, and has been a steady influence on American fashion for many years. Watching a Bill Blass collection is like a crash course in the American social scene. These are clothes for the jet set, who want clothes for New York, for gala balls in Washington, for resort wear, for international travel. He and Beene are the closest an American woman needs to get to the Paris couturiers. The fabrics are just as exclusive (Swiss textile leaders Abraham were deliriously happy that Blass used their fabrics for 75% of his spring collection). Blass is at his best with his crisply tailored fitted suits and his supremely glamorous sequinned dresses in Art Deco geometrics.

Whenever Liza Minnelli makes a stunning entrance at a gala opening, chances are she will be wearing a dress by Halston. This has never been a designer to play around with casual clothes. Even his resort wear has chic. You don't throw on a Halston, you wear it with style.

R. Halston Frowick from Indiana began his design career as a milliner in Chicago, then moved to New York at the invitation of the top store, Bergdorf Goodman. The fact that he was to switch over to more general fashion could well be due to his early days as student and assistant to Charles James.

Ironically, in a very hatty season, there was not a hat or even a hair decoration to be seen in this ex-milliners' collection for spring. But there were many traces of his early training from Charles James. It showed in the way his satin jersey dresses fold and drape, showing the

HALSTON

body to advantage. The couture background was revealed, too, in the way he used a one-lapel theme on jackets and coats, emphasising the long slim line of his day clothes. His evening dresses were layers of pearlised organza, strapless at the top, the skirts a narrowing petal shape, width coming only from the draped shoulders of the matching wraps.

Like any other fashion centre, New York has its cult figures. Way out in front is Mary McFadden, who turned from an interest in art, as a wealthy young lady with an equally

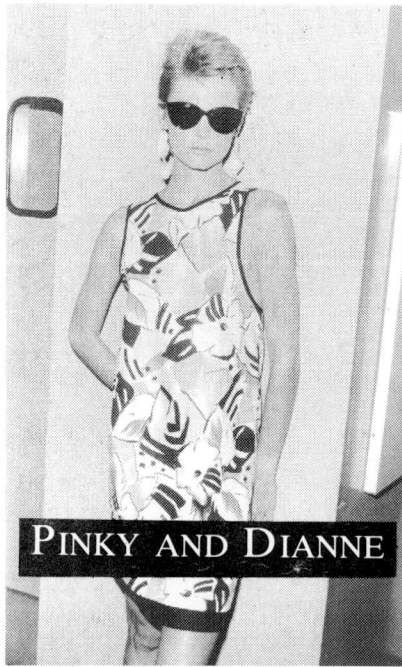

PINKY AND DIANNE

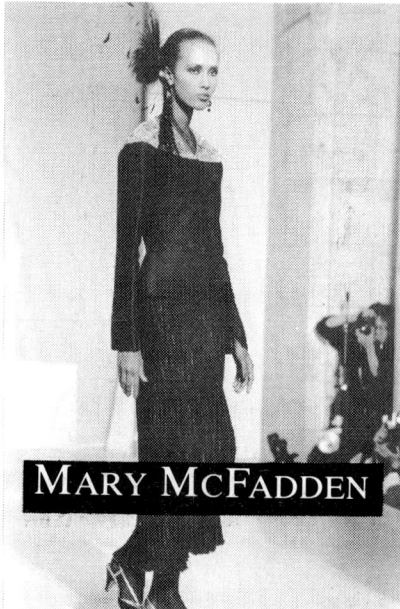

MARY MCFADDEN

well-endowed husband, to a career as a designer. She has her own, very individual style, using appliqués and unusual prints together with the crinkle silk associated with Fortuny. For spring she adopted the Islamic approach with Persian-inspired patterns, sumptuous sequinned cloths based on Turkish tiles, and a series in black and white using the Islamic arabesques. Her lamé evening dresses will become heirlooms.

Michaele Volbracht is a handsome young man with a background in graphics and great connections among American society. When

they needed a fashion show to help the appeal to restore the Central Park carousel, it was to Volbracht that they turned. His designers are somewhat eccentric, like his ricrac braided gipsy dresses, but he has style.

The purists can turn to Zoran, (who makes the kind of apparently simple shapes that turn out to be impossible to reproduce, yet look divine) and they have Ronaldus Shamask. He was trained as an architect and this sometimes leads to too much construction, but his spring collection, now that shape was back, had great appeal. He has something in common with Issey Miyake in his use of fabric, folding and stitching it into sculptured shapes. His colours were all neutral other than clear red and teal blue, and his signature for the season was the multi-layered folded square, used as collars and yokes, on square or melon-sleeved tunics.

Gloria Sachs is another of the stalwart American ladies who have been on the fashion scene for some time. In 1982 she was fêted as a great American designer by Lord & Taylor, the New York store which has

had a tradition for supporting American design since 1932, due to the influence of a great buyer called Dorothy Shaver. For spring Gloria Sachs ignored all talk of fit and short skirts. Her hems reached the ankles, her jackets were safari styles with peplums and for evening she used sarong wrapped and clinging animal printed silks.

Among the first of the younger stylists from the United States to reach Europe were two wildly dissimilar yet compatible girls called Pinky & Dianne. The girls met at the Washington University School of Fine Arts in St. Louis, where they both gained their Bachelor of Fine Arts degrees in 1967. Naturally, they made straight for New York where they each found jobs in Seventh Avenue. Since 1968 they have designed collections together, first as freelances and, by 1974, under their own label. Their interest in art showed through in their spring collection, with the post-modern Memphis Star designs, bold black and white prints cut into tubular dresses wth asymmetric and tiered hems. Another group in black and indigo or white glazed linen reflected an architectural feel in more constructed shapes, with the seams

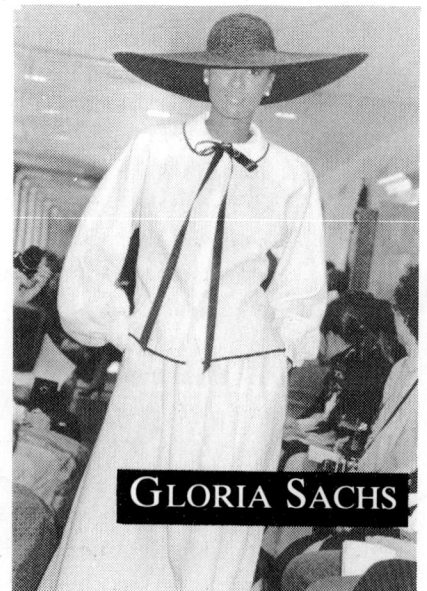

GLORIA SACHS

sewn to emphasise an "inside out" approach. There was also a pop art section, 60s prints in Courrèges shapes, which gave an uncomfortable feeling not only of déja vu, but of how did we ever wear it first time around?

Shape was news at Norma Kamali, who made her name with her young, dare we say it, kookie

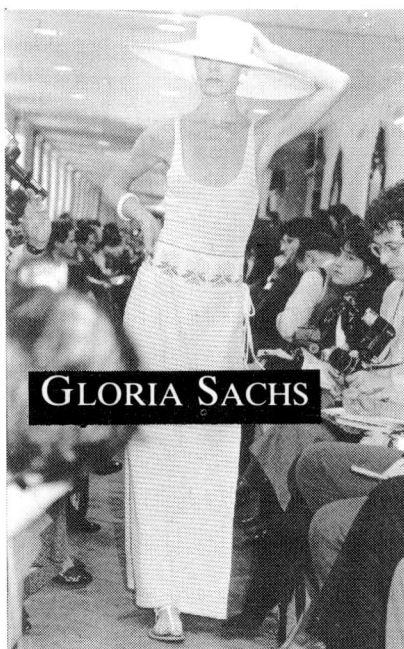

GLORIA SACHS

styles. Now she, along with her customers, is growing more mature but still has a sense of fun. She returned to denim, not stonewashed but what she calls "crisp crunchy" and cut it into big melon-sleeved jackets, oversized shirt tail dresses, sawn-off romper suits. To wear under them were longjohns in the now famous sweat shirt fabric, which she also used for riding jackets, blazers and tiny skirts.

Each season new names emerge. This spring saw a collection by Mary Anne Restivo, a designer who has been on Seventh Avenue for some years designing such things as Dior blouses. She has a way with softly wrapped dresses in silk fâconné, and fluid separates in gabardine and jersey, very much in the Anne Klein tradition. Fiandaca launched his

MARY ANNE RESTIVO

ready-to-wear, based on the couture styling he has been providing very happily for the ladies of Boston for some years. His sculptured evening dresses in pastel coloured organzas were equal to any of the international market.

There are surprisingly few black designers as yet in New York. An exception is Willi Smith, the bouncy, energetic designer at WilliWear who produces a young, commercial collection that can sell as well in Europe as in the United States. For spring he used cotton or linen for short cotton shifts with deep pastel pockets, and for the little dresses cut straight to a dropped seam, the bias flared with an asymmetric hem. His suits were big jacketed, wide trousered and in sets of checks, as far from Calvin Klein's chic city suits as you can imagine.

Such is the breadth, and excitement, of American fashion.●

VIVIENNE·WESTWOOD

LONDON

INTERNATIONAL INFLUENCE

● *By Sally Brampton*

London has for some time been regarded as the poor relation of the international fashion circuit. However that attitude is softened by a certain tolerant affection – how the mighty have fallen since the late and great days of the Swinging Sixties when London led the fashion world a merry dance and all others followed because only the English truly understood the steps.

Today, the powerful international buyers and press come to London not to buy, but to window shop. Designers the world over watch our unique and indigenous brand of eclectic eccentricity and, without a doubt, draw the ideas and turn them into money. In the 70s raw, savage punk became tame black leather and seductively tattered chiffon when it stalked onto the Paris catwalks; the ruffled New Romantics and pseudo–religious cults worshipped by the Blitz Club kids were transormed into chic Cavaliers resplendent in silk, satin and lace. In the early 80s it is the Japanese, seemingly set to take over fashion and the world, who openly acknowledge the debt of inspiration they owe to the street style of London.

Outrageously bizarre street fashion is a phenomenon peculiar to London. It occurs in other major cities but on a much subdued scale, and the original ideas are often rooted in the London scene. It is an advantage born of our disadvantages – the class system, poverty, lack of education and unemployment. The English are an eccentrically creative breed who, when they find no established focus for expression, explode violently into unconventional style, music and fashion.

The King's Road, twenty years on since the style explosion of the 60s, still jumps to the beat of a hundred native-born trends. The new punk, now a more brilliantly coloured bird than the menacing crow it was at birth, walks side by side with re-modernised Mods, bowler-hatted Hobos, Buffalo girls, spic zoot-suited boys and fifties belles. The look for early '83, and it was out of date even as the idea found expression, was dubbed 'Hard Times'. It required one pair of jeans, (style purists only wore Levi's 501's) ripped, torn, bleached and patched, worn over pristine indigo denims or cream wool grandad longjohns. Wild boys added ripped and torn American plaid shirts, classic white Brando t-shirts, black leather jackets or genuine (and they looked it) old Levi jackets and stout Doc Marten boots.

It was an easy look and cheap but its followers refused to acknowledge its roots in recession. Self-styled sociologist of the street, Perry Haines, said that it had more to do with Mad Max (biker-boy cult hero) than Mad Maggie (true–blue cult heroine) and a veteran of the club circuit remarked acidly that it was more to do with good old sex than good old poverty, "some boys just like to let their ass hang out".

To describe the London of the early 80s as a coherent fashion centre is a misnomer; it is a style centre that houses a number of independents who all have their own very individual labels. Of these the most truly individual is Vivienne Westwood. An original of her time, she scoffs at the idea of contrived individualism, "either you have it or you don't", ignores conventional fashion directions and simply goes her own sweet way; a way that others the world over have followed.

Affectionately known as the grandmother of punk, she launched a million frilly pirate shirts with the Buccaneer collection and turned underwear into outerwear when she produced Buffalo girls wearing neon-satin Sweater Girl Bras over rough wool tunic tops – a sight that stopped more than one

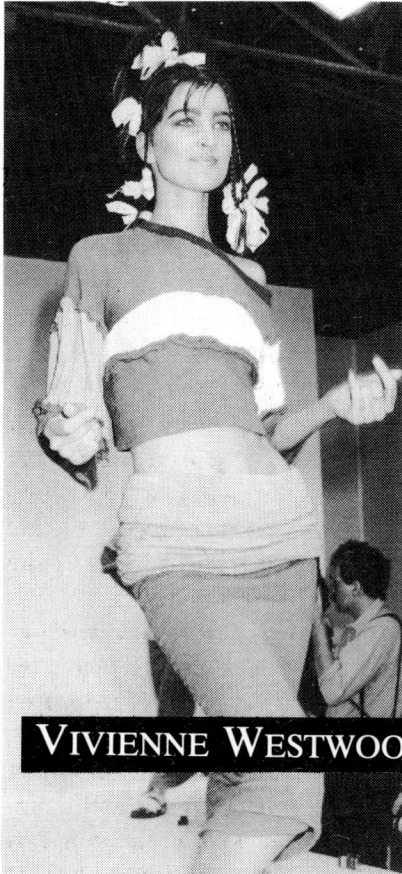

VIVIENNE WESTWOOD

VIVIENNE WESTWOOD

unsuspecting tourist dead in their tracks in the summer of '82.

Her design is evolutionary and revolutionary. Last spring she took punk back to the drawing board, coloured it up and called it punk couture or 'Punkature'. Her ideas, often a jumble sale of inspiration at first sight, have become absorbed in conventional ideas of dress. Intentionally twisted seams, intentionally badly-cut clothes, intentionally unfinished hems and deliberate contradictions of colour have all challenged established dictums.

She is inarticulate and impatient about her creativity but believes that culture reflects society and fashion must be one of its showcases. As she is frustrated to the point of anarchy: "I just want to fuck everything up"; her clothes are aimed as a direct blow at the system but a blow that paradoxically becomes absorbed and embraced by it, to the point that the chain-store multiples produce rail after rail of diluted Westwood.

That fails to irritate her; she seems oblivious of her impact. "Am I an influence? I suppose I am since a lot of people say so," and is more concerned with her present and future task of designing clothes that create some sort of ethic in total opposition to what she sees as the hypocrisy of the class system. Whatever her reasoning it will no doubt be lost in time leaving only the visual residue to mark her influence as surely as the bum-flapped bondage trousers and ripped slogan t-shirts with which she stamped 'punk' on the 70s.

The London designers have never lacked unconventional, creative energy. What has perhaps been lacking for so long is slick professionalism. The Americans, brilliant marketeers and promotionalists pointed the way into the hard-bitten commercial world of the 80s, and while Europe quickly picked up her skirts and followed suit, London had first to cut the umbilical cord of the 60s. The English have always been astonishingly good at ruling a world that exists only in their minds and other's memories (vestiges of the Empire still infiltrate this tiny island). When the swinging sixties became the anonymous seventies it was a change that the Great British designers were ill equipped to deal with.

The youth revolution of the 60s exploded most of the established fashion dictums and left an aftermath of unprofessionalism in which the British fashion industry has been floundering for more than a decade. The days of bright young things with bright young money were long gone, only the heritage of an arrogance that demanded unqualified recognition remained. There were exceptions; the de-

VIVIENNE WESTWOOD

MARGARET HOWELL

signers like Jean Muir, Zandra Rhodes and Janice Wainwright who moved with the times and quietly but effectively continue to make their mark with their own distinctively personal signatures.

To the new breed of designers, the 60s have only the relevance of history, and the irritating habit of being extolled, like a self-satisfied older brother, as the time when London was really great. London will be great again, but only on their terms. Stephen Linard, who in the two years since he started his business has turned from the angry, arrogant young man of art school to become a new designer with a convincingly strong direction, believes that London still has a hard lesson to learn.

"There has to be a more professional attitude, designers will have to start taking their business seriously and stop treating it as a trendy pastime. Only the best and the toughest will survive and the Kensington Market two-bit designers will die out. It's the end of all those one-night clubs and one-week designers." Linard feels that it is the inheritance of fast ideas and fast clothes that gave London a bad name in the 70s. "There are too many raw ideas here that never got followed through. In London once you've even thought of an idea then it's dead."

His ideas, which often sound pretty extraordinary at conception, (woollen scarves with sick stains actually knitted into them) follow through to a well-designed end-product (woollen scarves with tasteful, flecked patterns). He left fashion school amidst a standing ovation after a collection called 'Reluctant Emigrés'. It was an extraordinary mixture of the conventional and the shocking; beautifully cut and tailored trousers with a contrast patch in the most private of parts, and formal dress shirts made in sheer organza or chiffon worn by rough boys sporting tattoos on bulgeing biceps. His spring '83 collection, 'Angels with Dirty Faces', was inspired by the America of the depression-ridden 30s.

He used washed-out faded chintz patterned fabrics to make new dresses look like old, "good finds in a jumble sale," and showed them on hard, punky girls sporting bovver boots and tattoos. His skimpy bias-cut frocks were intended to look like the badly-cut reproductions that the big stores in the 30s copied from Paris originals, and which, by the time they arrived in the American mid-west were travesties of the original. He showed these hitched at the hip with trailing hems and slovenly, slouched shoulder straps but has no illusions about how they will eventually be worn by most: "just plain pretty, but then again I want everyone to wear my clothes. That's why I'm in the business."

This business-like attitude and hard-headed professionalism is exemplified in no other young designer as strongly as it is in the diminutive figure of Jasper Conran. Barely 22, he has done much to establish the reputation of the new breed of daywear designers and together with others like Sheridan Barnett, Maxfield Parrish and Margaret Howell is slowly abolishing the idea that London is only a city of fancy dressing. His attitude embraces none of the self-indulgent 'artistic' pretensions of the past, he sees fashion in the broader, pragmatic terms of an industry. "We must build this country into a strength. One of the reasons that the Europeans are so successful is because they co-operate – the designers, the manufacturers and the fabric mills all work together."

He is taking some steps to

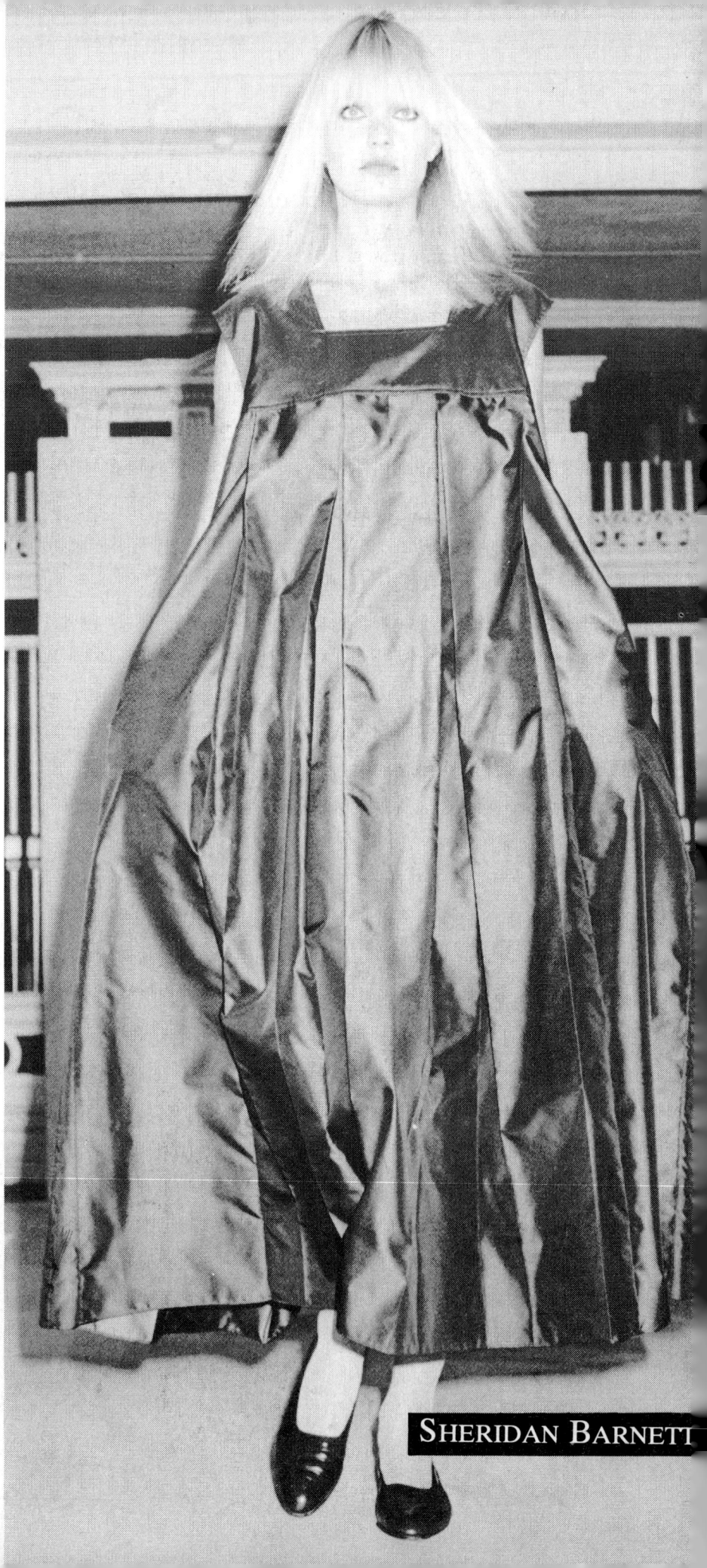

SHERIDAN BARNETT

establish that approach as the norm with a British-made shoe collection, a glove collection and many other plans for British-made franchises. He is a great believer in designing clothes that women will want to wear and has little time for showy gimmicks. His clothes are simple and uncluttered, tailored suits and separates that suit the modern woman perfectly.

He sees no point in putting clothes on the catwalk that will never be sold, "if you want to do fancy dress than go and be a costume designer," and thinks that the big catwalk shows are a thing of the past. "What's the point? You might fool the press; you might fool the buyers; but you won't fool the

JASPER CONRAN

public." To him the traditional English look is the epitome of style, "where did Chanel get her classic tweed cardigans from?" but believes that it is a heritage that we have failed to capitalise on as yet.

Designers all over the world emulate the English look, but no other race has ever done it as well as the English themselves. The tradition of tweeds and cashmere was lost for a while when the London designers busied themselves with silk and satin until Margaret Howell quietly re-

established the tradition, giving the stiff-upper lip of British tailoring a modern, more relaxed image.

Her big, loose jackets and box-pleated skirts, finely striped soft cotton shirts and brilliant Fair Isle sweaters were so successful that Americans would arrive in her tiny London shop, straight off the transatlantic aeroplane, to part with a few thousand dollars before collapsing in their hotel rooms from jet-lag. This year she took pity on them and has opened shops in New York and Tokyo. Her style is instantly recognisable, supremely tailored, and devotees refer to her clothes as 'old friends' for they have the comfortable charm and endearing grace that is always affectionately described as 'English'.

Sheridan Barnett is another London designer with a sure direction towards which he heads with uncompromising dedication. He has always advocated simplicity and ease in his clothing, designs with an eye that is almost architectural in its purity and believes in adding no ornamentation or extraneous detail to distract from those clean-cut lines. His greatest love is menswear – on women; which is perhaps why his enormous linen trench coats, big

JASPER CONRAN

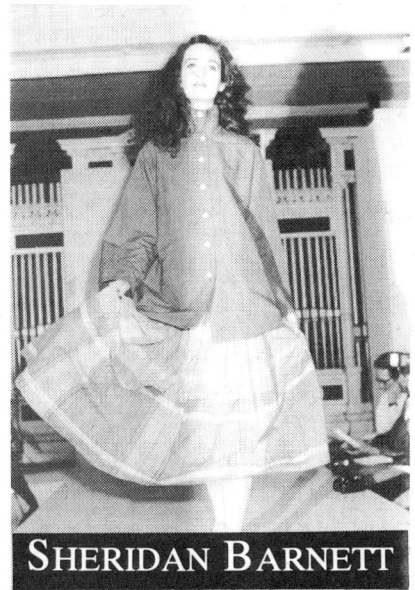

SHERIDAN BARNETT

loose jackets and fluid crêpe de Chine pyjamas have the same uncontrived but distinctive air that good men's clothes always bear. His spring collection was based on a long, full silhouette in shadowy, neutral tones of grey, smokey brown and rich cream, mixing linens with roughly textured cottons, slippery satins and thick, corded knits.

Nigel Preston of Maxfield Parrish shows the same confident handling of the butter soft suedes with which he established his name. He handles the skins as if they were the softest of wools and last spring produced a collection of big, loose coats and jackets in inky blues, faded rose and peachy beige swept over soft, fluid skirts and comfortable, cropped pants. His newest technique was to overlap skins in a neutral patchwork and cut this textured effect into square, geometrical shifts, tops and tubular skirts which wrapped at the waist or hips like sarongs.

The enormous wave of creative energy and the growing numbers of talented young designers indicate that London, at the beginning of the 80s cannot fairly be labelled as the poor relation of the international fashion circuit, but simply the quiet one.●

JAPAN

● *By Geraldine Ranson*

In October 1982 something very exciting happened. As if by one accord the buyers and press attending the French ready-to-wear previews of fashion for the following spring, realised that there was a new dimension in Paris. There were not just Japanese designers showing among the French as there had been for more than a decade; they were witnessing the emergence of a separate Japanese school of fashion.

Many who were closely involved in international fashion had seen it coming. European designers had mentioned Japan again and again as an influence. In London Sheridan Barnett was transfixed by a Japanese woman he saw in Regent Street dressed in many shades of grey. She inspired his successful autumn 1982 collection. But what had happened to world fashion to persuade 12 Japanese designers to show their collections in Paris? After all, they have 125 million Japanese in their home market who are more receptive to fashion and to change than many Westerners.

Paris first became aware of Japanese design when Kenzo Takada launched his sparkling young collection in Paris in 1970. In less than a decade he was one of the most copied and influential designers in the world. In 1966 a more important event had occurred. Yves Saint-Laurent had launched his ready-to-wear collection and within a few years there were Rive Gauche boutiques across the world. Between the two of them they put paid to Paris couture as the source of world fashion.

Soon the prêt-à-porter had taken over from the couture as the centre of excitement in Paris. Sonia Rykiel, Dorothée Bis and Emmanuelle Khanh led the field. And then, in the mid-seventies, three designers came to the fore: Karl Lagerfeld designing for Chloé, Claude Montana and Thierry Mugler. French fashion took another turn. Ready-to-wear had appeared as a response to the mood of the times. Women were too busy to stand for fittings for made-to-measure clothes. Both Kenzo's Jap collection and Yves Saint-Laurent's Rive Gauche were factory made. But the Chloé, Montana and Mugler main collections were of a quality that demanded all the individual skills of couture production. As Gabrielle Aghion, Vice President of Chloé, told me recently: "Our production is exactly like couture. The only difference is that our customers do not have fittings." Between them, Lagerfeld, Montana and Mugler took the lead away from the ready-to-wear industry. The field was left open, the Japanese saw their opportunity and their leading designers flew to Paris to show their collections.

When I visited Tokyo last November, I found many Japanese sceptical about Western acceptance of their fashion. They pointed out that whenever the West has lacked talent or inspiration of its own, it has turned to the East for renewal. Others were more optimistic for their own success. They believe that much Western fashion still harks back to the leisured life-style of the rich minority before the Second World War, that this fashion has little to offer the working woman of today and that the clothes do not match the backdrop of our homes, our offices and indeed our whole lives. Having read these words you might expect to arrive in Japan and find the local women dressed in their own distinctive and modern style. You would be disappointed. There are as many Sloane Rangers on the streets of Tokyo as in Knightsbridge and it is rare to see a woman wearing a kimono other than at a wedding or formal party. Today Japanese girls attend night school to learn how to tie an obi, the 13 ft. long sash that is worn with the traditional dress.

KENZO

Japanese women love the idea of the status that famous designer labels are all supposed to bestow and Burberry, Gucci, Missoni, Emmanuelle Khanh *et al* do good business there. Yet today the Japanese are beginning to value their own creativity.

Once a Japanese designer had to establish his reputation in the West before he could hope for recognition at home. Issey Miyake, today one of the most popular designers in Japan, went straight from University in Japan to Paris to study at the design school of La Chambre Syndicale de la Couture Parisienne. He presented his first collection under his own label in Paris in 1973 and has continued to do so ever since.

Chie Koike who today is the professor in charge of Bunka College of Fashion in Tokyo recalls with pride that she was at La Chambre Syndicale school in the same year's course as Yves Saint Laurent and that Karl Lagerfeld was in the year behind her. Chie Koike and others like her, with their down-to-earth approach to fashion, have contributed enormously to the success of the Japanese home industry and its reputation for efficiency and quality. At Bunka all students must

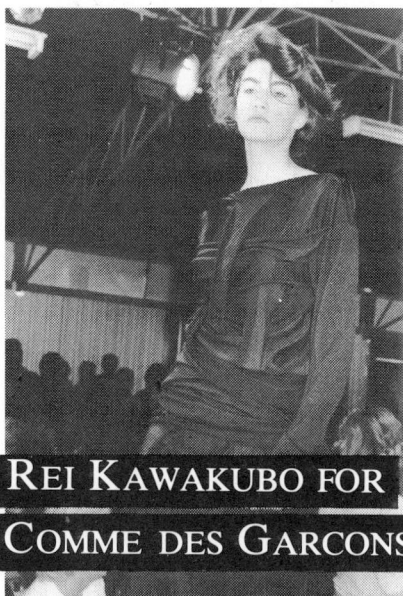

REI KAWAKUBO FOR COMME DES GARCONS

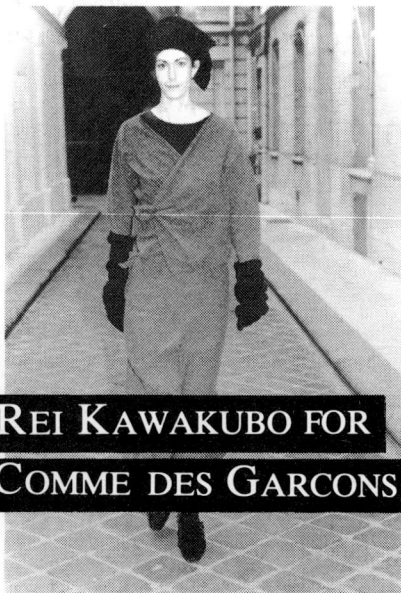

REI KAWAKUBO FOR COMME DES GARCONS

take the general two or three year courses in all aspects of clothing production. Only a very few go on to the one year design course. Bunka aims to produce many more clothing technicians than designers, unlike most British art schools which have a reputation for turning out many talented designers whose only weakness is lack of technical expertise. Graduation photographs around the professor's walls included one with Junko Koshino, Kenzo, and the designers who today work for Nicole, Pink House and My Make – all leading manufacturers.

Back in the 1950s, when Japan was beginning to recover from the Second World War, Hanae Mori opened a studio in Tokyo to design costumes for films. With American influence sweeping Japan and a demand for Western-style clothes, she soon developed a private clientele who were later the first customers of her couture house. Now 57, she has homes and showrooms in New York and in Paris where her salon shares Rue Montaigne with Christian Dior, Emanuel Ungaro and Guy Laroche. At home in Tokyo she owns 15 companies including Studio V, a

factory producing young wholesale fashion, run by her youngest son, Kei.

When I returned from Tokyo, I sat down to write my report for *The Sunday Telegraph* in a state of great trepidation. I knew that the pictures I had brought back must strike most of the readers as bizarre, or even outrageous, but that I had to report an important departure in fashion. Here is what I wrote:-

"Yohji Yamamoto and Rei Kuwakubo, two Japanese designers barely known in the West, are leading a new movement which will change the way we think about fashion, and, ultimately the way we dress. Few of us will yet want to wear their clothes but through their influence on other designers across the world they will surely reach us."

These two designers, both graduates of the prestigious Keio University and close friends in their private lives, are 40 and 41 respectively. Both have tried to produce clothes that will fulfil the same function for women that men's clothes have for many years performed for men. For the first time designers are producing clothing that does not start from the premise of women as sex objects. Not everyone can accept it.

Kuwakubo is a philosophy graduate who has had no formal design training. To meet her surrounded by her staff, all dressed in black in the clothes that she designs for Comme des Garçons, is to undergo instant conversion to her style. She is tiny and slim with an intelligent humorous face. She never wears make-up and like so many Japanese women who never seem to show their age, she could be 15 or 50. For the last 10 years Rei says that her taste for everything black and white has remained unchanged. She never uses prints and prefers to concentrate on texture. Her much-

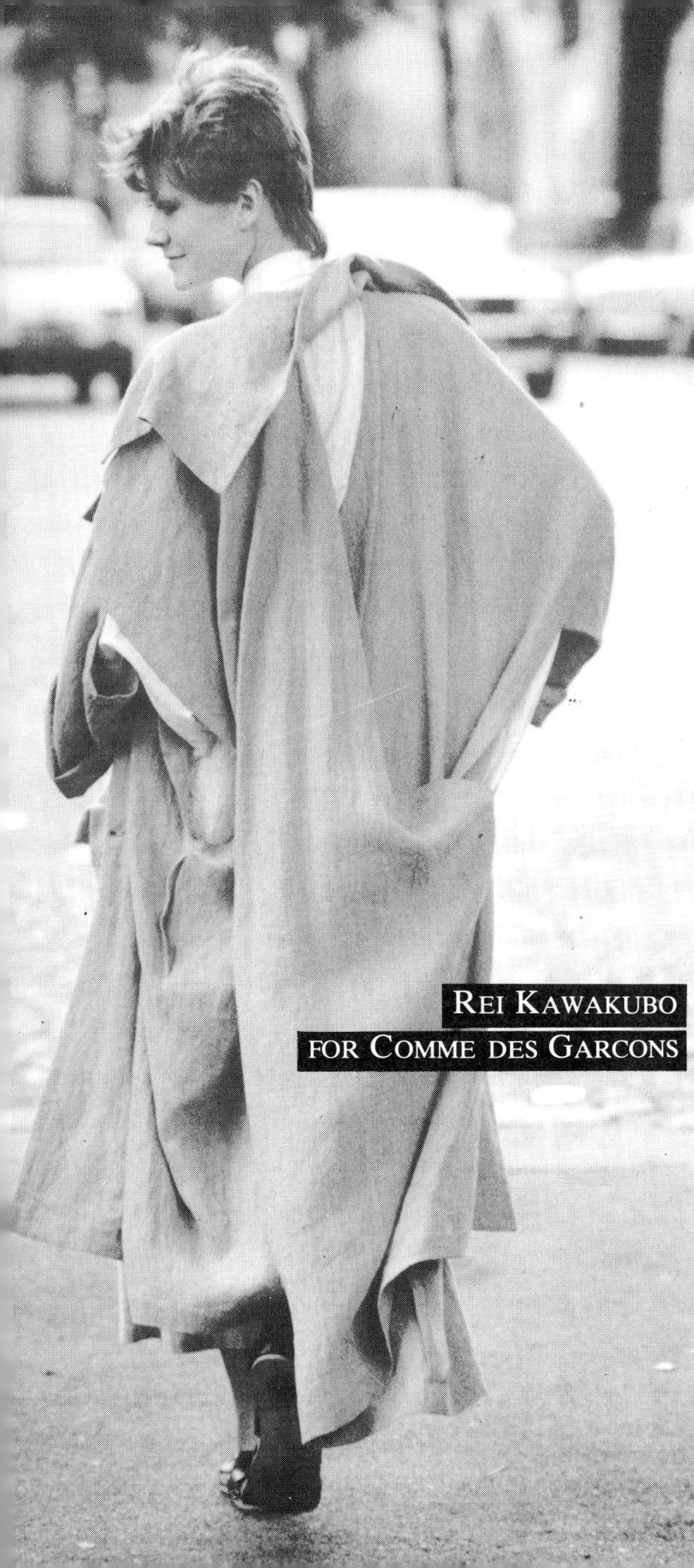

REI KAWAKUBO FOR COMME DES GARCONS

criticised 'rags', or the dresses which she slashes and stitches are examples of how she adds texture to a plain flat fabric. These dresses always have a lining as no Japanese women would wear anything see-through or revealing. When I questioned Rei about one of the jackets in her collection she was amused: "You are not so safe emotionally in a jacket without a back," she replied. "But if it worries you, think of it as an apron."

I had been told in Tokyo that Rei was a tough feminist but she dismissed her critics thus: "Most men don't like women who are capable of working hard. They do not like strong, independent women with their feet on the ground," She would be pleasantly surprised she said if a man outside the fashion industry liked her collection, but she would not expect him to understand it. "It's not cute or soft and it doesn't fit a man's image of a woman. Men don't want women to be outstanding."

Yohji Yamamoto describes himself as a nomad. He is fragile-looking with long hair for a Japanese and a thin, straight black beard. He has a distinctive and vivid face lit by a frequent smile. Yohji, or Y as he is called, produces one inexpensive young range of clothing with the following words written in English on the label: "There is nothing so boring as a neat and tidy look." It tells us a great deal about what fashion has been trying to communicate during the last decade. Although he is one of the most articulate Japanese designers, Yamamoto believes that he is too enmeshed in the new fashion movement to be truly objective. He makes working clothes that are never showy and believes that it is the function of literature, and not fashion, to communicate inner feelings. Like

53

JUNKO KOCHINO

and stayed. Today her original young Michiko collections are manufactured in both Japan and in Italy and when I was in Tokyo she shared a fashion show with her sister Junko Koshino. The older sister, Hiroko Koshino, showed separately, but all three joined together for a gala show in Osaka.

Members of the public can usually buy tickets for trade fashion shows in Japan for about the same price as a seat in the stalls in a London theatre. Clearly they enjoy

most Japanese designers, he makes no evening clothes. Y travels for inspiration and, like Kenzo, gambles for excitement. Now he is successful he finds it hard to remain outside the fashion establishment: "But I keep working at it," he says with a grin.

For anyone interested in fashion, Tokyo offers the opportunity to visit the Kabuki theatre and to see the traditional sets and costumes that have such a strong influence on Japanese designers. All the actors

are men and the young apprentices often crouch on the stage in their traditional black uniform with its hood and mask to tidy the sets or rearrange an actor's costume. Kansai Yamamoto dressed in the same Kabuki black, has often adopted this tactic himself in his Paris fashion shows.

In 1973 Michiko Koshino came to London to seek her fortune in a city where she would not be overshadowed by her talented older sisters. She married an Englishman

54

the spectacle and Yukiko Hanai's Madame Hanai collection was a local favourite. Not all the stars of Tokyo Fashion Week bring their collections to Paris and one of the highlights of my visit was Mitsuhiro Matsuda's collection for Nicole. (It is interesting to reflect that the same collection sells under the French name, Nicole, in Japan and under the designer's name, Matsuda, in the West.) The big gymnasium at Bunka college was packed to see Matsuda's creative, original and yet very wearable menswear and many of the best women's styles drew on the same inspiration. Another fine collection that is not shown in Europe is Yoshie Inaba's for Bigi. European buyers who cannot get to Tokyo, sometimes buy Nicole and Bigi in New York.

As the West has its own resident Japanese designers so Tokyo has its Europeans. Jurgen Lehl, a 39-year-old West German, has worked in Tokyo since 1970, first designing fabrics and then, since 1974, his own

YOHJI YAMAMOTO

ready-to-wear collection with today his own accessories, sheets, towels and furnishing fabrics. He says that he is only just ready to export but that he will never show his collection in Paris. Spurning modern office blocks, Lehl has his headquarters in a warehouse with a view across the Tokyo harbour water. He clearly thrives in the Japanese environment: "You can sell anything new here as long as it is practical. Japan is moving fast and the people are changing too. The shops in the towns in the provinces here are my best customers. The people are less stuffy and they love colour." Lehl's collection included some impressive knitwear and a novel idea of buttoning, rather than seaming, his dresses along the joins.

Freight, tariffs and the cost of buyers' travel to Japan often combine to place the price of Japanese fashion beyond the reach of many women in the West. Yet if we accept that imitation is the greatest praise, Japanese designers need only have visited the French mass-market fashion fair at the Porte de Versailles in Paris in the spring of 1983, just six months after they first won such acclaim, to see the magnitude of their influence. ●

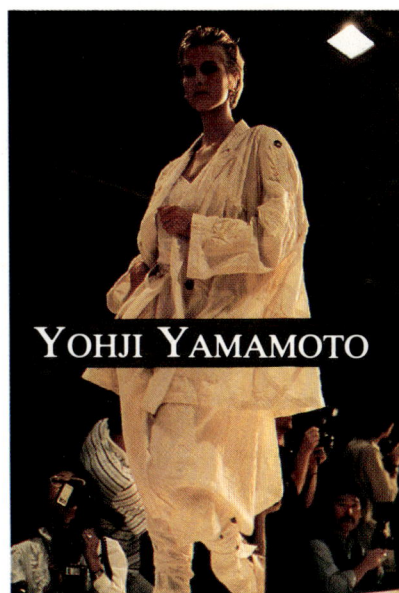

KANSAI YAMAMOTO

ISSEY MIYAKE

THE ILLUSIONIST

● *By Brenda Polan*

Five years ago, in the introduction to Issey Miyake's book, *East Meets West*, Diana Vreeland, fashion's own grande dame, wrote: "His clothes are totally his and his alone." She then went on, slightly incoherently but with much truth: "I love you, Issey, and the way you carry on and on and on, from your centuries old traditions, down through the ages, utilising your total instinct and great integrity to present artistry and beautiful inspirations that are so well applied to the present-tense of East and West."

Miyake's vision is unique. So is his creative imagination and his technical expertise with both cloth and cut. He is one of the designers most watched and admired by other designers and his influence upon a whole generation of designers, predominantly Japanese but also European, has been formidable. He it was who shattered design preconceptions and explored new concepts and techniques, always soundly based in traditional craft, thus making possible the controversial new wave of Japanese designers whose work has, perforce, dominated 1983.

Born in 1935, Miyake studied art at Tama University in Tokyo where he designed his first collection in 1963. He graduated in 1964 and moved to Paris in the following year to study design at the school of the Chambre Syndicale de la Couture Parisienne, leaving in 1966 to work as an assistant designer at Guy Laroche, the couture house.

Thus he was in Paris when the workers occupied the Renault plant and the students took to the streets, manning the modern-day barricades of burnt-out trams and dustbins and digging up the cobblestones to fling at the tear-gas toting riot police. For Issey, as for everyone else involved, it was a traumatic period.

His friend, the architect Arata Isozaki, reported: "I am not certain whether or not he had already formed his own critical opinion of haute couture, a staunchly regulated genre of international fashion. However, finding himself in Paris, a city full of suspicion and jealousy, faced by a language barrier which handicapped his liberty, he probably saw no reason to remain where he was, and thus, he took flight.

"One of the characteristics of the protest movement was impulsive body action; energy was burnt. After that, in the vacuum, the question loomed once again in front of him: 'As a designer, what are clothes?'"

Miyake's flight, physically at least, did not take him far and, once peace was restored to the streets of Paris, he went to work in the studio of another great couturier, Hubert de Givenchy. His ideas had, however, fled far. The posed formality of the haute couture approach to dressing which was still, with the exception of Courrèges' sculptured space-age mini tunics, all Paris had to offer women, seemed antipathetic and out of step. Revolution was in the air and haute couture was, to those sensitive to these things, suddenly rather *ancien régime*.

So, in 1969, Issey Miyake took himself off to a city somewhat less set in its ways, New York. He worked as a designer for Geoffrey Beene, producing ready-to-wear clothes and enjoying the heady atmosphere of the city. He was also refining his ideas about dress and the function of fashion. The result was his theory of "peeling away to the limit", throwing away all the inhibiting ideas about dress imposed by Western cultural imperialism, and starting again from the beginning – the bolt of cloth, its nature and its potential.

He returned to Tokyo in 1970 to make his ideas

concrete. At first his clothes consisted of pieces of irregularly shaped fabric almost suspended around the body, each piece of which could be stripped away to reveal another part of the body. He quickly moved into layering and wrapping and his unparallelled feeling for texture, mass and volume became evident. He himself attributes much of his thinking to the influence of Madeleine Vionnet who, in 1920s Paris, attempted to take clothing back to the basic shapes dictated by the qualities of the fabric. She did not cut fabric and then stitch it so that it fitted the body; instead, she used the body as an under-frame along the lines of which the fabric hung, draped and flowed effortlessly, naturally, assuming new shapes as the body moved.

This concept Miyake developed in ways magical to watch on the runway, creating garments of what appeared to be dramatic simplicity itself by which, at the twitch of the model's shoulder, suddenly became something else entirely – something equally simple, equally dramatic. During the seventies, while still based in Tokyo, Miyake began to show his collection twice a year in Paris and they rapidly became shows no fashion addict could afford to miss.

Miyake's skill with fabric is rooted in his knowledge of traditional Japanese fabrics and fabric-production techniques. The ascendancy of denim in the sixties and seventies turned his attention to Japanese workwear fabrics: ticking stripe, heavy cottons, quilting. These he incorporated into his work both in their original form and in wonderfully elaborated forms,

■ *Catwalk pictures of Miyake's Autumn/Winter 1983 Collections as seen in Paris*

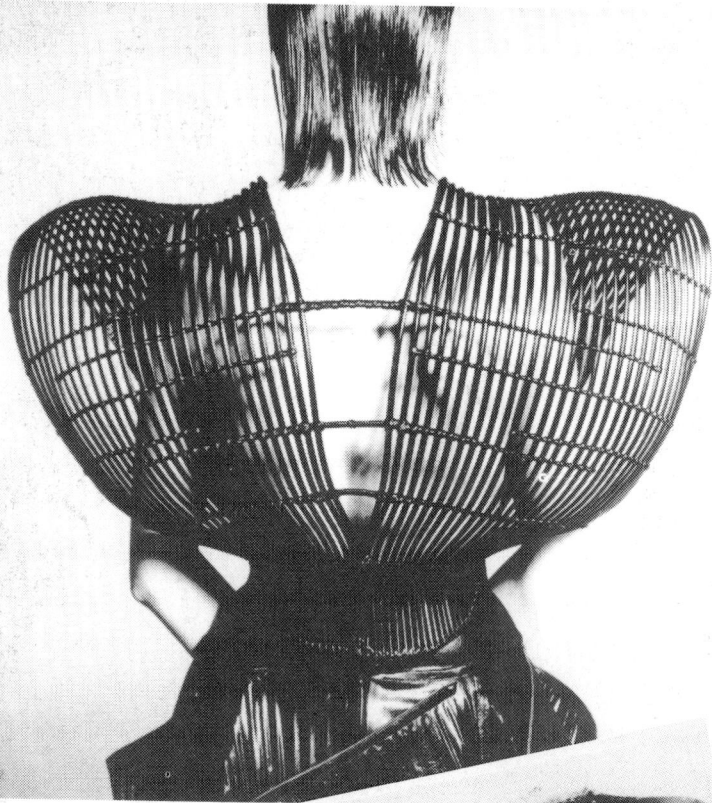

waffle textures, heavy coarse weaves, open-mesh weaves, rich seersucker effects, wrinkled, crinkled, primitive pleated, occasionally smocked. Combined with Miyake's sophisticated colour sense, the effect of all this sensuous texture was completely fresh. Textured fabrics, when employed by other designers, tended to be conventionally rich – velvet, plain, panne or printed, brocade, damask, corduroy or appliqué work, embroidery or lace, nubbled or hairy tweed; even when used in fresh, unexpected ways by great designers like Yves Saint Laurent and Kenzo Takada, they were clothing clichés.

It is not, of course, in the nature of fabrics like the ones Miyake has developed to respond well to being intricately cut, seamed, darted, fitted. And that is consistent with his vision. "I like," he says, "to work in the spirit of the kimono. Between the body and the fabric there exists only an approximate contact."

He does not use the kimono itself as many Western designers do, to add a touch of exoticism. He merely borrows its attributes of ease, adaptability and respect for the fabric and the patterns and shapes in space which it can create when the body moves. "This makes it possible," he says, "to appreciate the beauty of both the fabric and of the human body and, in addition, the beauty of the harmony that can be created when both are allowed expression."

If he sounds serious about his design philosophy, well, he is. But he also has a rich sense of humour which contributes substantially to his famous charm. He loves to make

■ *Clockwise from top left, 1982, 1976, 1976, 1974. Right: Autumn/Winter 1983*

outrageous overstatements on the runway, sending on his models spinning like tops in multi-coloured grass skirts of mega-proportions, or clad in shiny fibreglass breastplates complete with tip-tilted 1950s breasts and perky nipples or polished wickerwork torso cages shaped like extravagant versions of samurai armour.

His sense of theatre is unequalled among contemporary designers. In 1976 he presented Issey Miyake and Twelve Black Girls, using a dozen of America's most strikingly Amazonian models, which played for six days in Osaka and was seen by 15,000 people. Next year he mounted Fly With Issey Miyake and a total of 22,000 people in Tokyo and Kyoto watched it. His book, *East Meets West,* produced by his own Design Studio in Tokyo, is lavishly illustrated and treasured by everyone in the fashion industry lucky enough to own it. In 1980 he moved, not too surprisingly, into theatre design, producing the costumes for Maurice Béjart's ballet, *Casta Diva.*

Miyake produces his own-name range plus Issey Sport, somewhat cheaper, and Plantation, a pared down, almost jokey and very youthful range. It was in the Plantation range that he managed to find a use for a crinkled thick paper fabric which has been used for peasant workwear in Japan for 250 years.

He is, without doubt, one of the great innovators in the history of fashion and although his compatriots of somewhat lesser talent might outrage with their "post-Hiroshima" or beggarwoman look, the genius who cleared the space for them to launch it will always only outrage as he amuses. And that kind of pleasure is rare in fashion. ●

KARL LAGERFELD

THE LEADER

● *By Suzy Menkes*

When Chanel showed to the press on 25th January, there was a frisson of excitement in the narrow, formal salon not felt since the great Mademoiselle herself had died 12 years earlier.

Up the grand staircase surged a crowd of famous faces: Paloma Picasso in black leather and snap-fastened sweats, elegant actresses Dominique Sanda and Isabelle Adjani; a row of Rothschilds, two rows of ambassadors wives, ex-first lady Mme Pompidou.

They had come, we had all come, to see what Karl had done with Chanel. Karl Lagerfeld, the self-styled 'fashion machine' had taken on the burden of fashion history at Chanel couture, *as well as* continuing to design for the house of Chloé, for the Fendis in Rome and even for several other collections of separates and accessories.

Where Karl leads others trail behind. He was the first to create for Chloé what the French call *le flou:* fluid, feminine dresses with all hems, and linings banished. He scented the romantic revival and sent out models dressed like eighteenth century Dresden shepherdesses. (The eighteenth century, its rococo furnishings and flourishes are his first love. And at one time he played out the part of eighteenth century courtier in frock coat, brocade waistcoat, fan and pony tail). He still has the pony tail and the fans (another passion). "But I collect them only to use them," he says. "I abhor the idea of collecting things to put away." The Chanel couture collection was his first attempt at haute couture. With typical flourish, he started his transformation by making over Mademoiselle's famous rooms in the rue Cambon – and then played a visual trick on us all by taking the Japanese screens that were the most famous part of Chanel's own decor, and turned them into exquisite embroideries in the collection.

Wit is a crucial part of the Lagerfeld style. His Chloé collections are peppered with amusing accessories – an evening bag patterned with black and white musical notes, or a dress with two taps embroidered at the shoulder blades and a whole shower of sequins pouring down the derrière. The ideas flow so fast that in each (200 plus garments) collection, there are many different themes and silhouettes. He was frustrated by the slowness of haute couture, willing the Chanel workroom to speed up the painstaking process of creation.

If he thinks as fast as he speaks, it is not surprising that he is a creative force. His voice is a stacatto bleep, with the slight guttural sounds and glottal stops of his native Germany. He speaks fluently French, German, Italian, English on the same toneless note.

"I am a kind of fashion computer," he says. "Or maybe you can say that I am an image-maker. No, I am a vampire. When I work with Carla Fendi she has an idea and I suck it out of her."

His relationship with Carla Fendi is crucial to his work. He has worked with the Fendis for 16 years, during which they have together created new boundary lines about what can be achieved in fur. The last collection was an extraordinary *tour de force,* a wild celebration of the animal side of fur, with skins ravaged and tattered and mixed in unlikely combinations (mongolian lamb with skunk, possum with weasel) and even stained with blood red dye.

"I was just thinking," says Karl insouciantly, "of a few splashes of wine."

The curtains in his eighteenth century mansion on the Left Bank of Paris are blood red. The salon is ice blue brocade, with gilding decorating chairs, tables, pictures, mirrors. It is lunchtime, and the entire house is lit by candles.

But if this is the real Karl Lagerfeld, there are still other facets of his taste and character. He has his apartment in Rome, his studio in the Rue de Rivoli where he does most of his designing with his assistant and protegé, Hervé Leger. Then there is the flat in Monte Carlo, his "official" home (he is a tax exile). It is decorated in the witty, fifties-inspired post modern style of the Milanese Memphis team. Or at least it was at the time of writing. Karl Lagerfeld changes décor as often as he changes the fashion images of his collections. No wonder that one of his close friends is interior designer Andrée Putman.

Lagerfeld's other homes (or perhaps they should simply be called 'properties') are his lakeside villa in Switzerland and his château in Britanny, one or other of which was left to him by an aunt and he feels a faint family duty to hang on to it.

■ *Above: Lagerfeld for Chanel couture collection, spring/summer. Right and far right: Chloé, spring/summer*

Even if Karl Lagerfeld did not earn two and a half million dollars a year from his share in his best-selling Chloé perfume (backed by Elizabeth Arden) he would be a very wealthy man (reputed total income over five million dollars). His father was Scandinavian, but built up his dairy empire in Hamburg. Karl was born to luxury. "I was always interested in clothes. One of my earliest memories was telling my valet to iron the collar of my shirt." His glamorous and slightly eccentric mother dragged her small son to Paris and round the couture houses, where he vividly remembered being riveted as a schoolboy by Chanel. "Then the clothes were very colourful and modern and funny," he says wistfully.

He left his Hamburg home and came to Paris at the age of 14. Two years later he was selected out of 200,000 entrants in a design competition sponsored by the International Wool Secretariat. The other joint winner was the shy young Yves Saint Laurent.

Lagerfeld learned his craft in the ateliers of the great couturiers in postwar Paris, especially at Balmain and Patou. Designer Roland Klein who worked as Karl's assistant at Patou recalls him then as an immensely amusing companion, a renaissance figure fascinated by painting, music, opera, poetry. Today he is still bound by the larger world of general culture, rather than the minutiae of the fashion world. He says now that he has no time for theatre, for the opera, for socializing (although he is somehow seen around at fashionable gatherings with his close friends, like Anna Piaggi from Italy or socialities like Ira Furstenberg).

He is not a 'social' person, in the sense of those in the fashion world who function and flourish at public gatherings. But neither does he seem

insists. "The whole creative progress is not an ego trip for me. I am not interested in making a name for myself."

This is both the strength and the weakness of his designing. At his most inspired, his collections are balanced, harmonious, truly elegant and refined in the French sense. 'Raffiné' describes that blend of style and chic which is strictly Parisian territory.

Yet can anyone recognize a Chloé 'look'? There is each season a line, or shape or theme that spells out the label to the initiated. But often Lagerfeld himself superimposes this like a badge of style. I remember the ridiculously wide corselet belt as the signature of a collection. Take that away, (and nobody actually wore them) and you had a series of marvellously elegant but quite unremarkable dresses. Saint Laurent has stamped his man-tailored, sportswear style on our fashion epoch. Chanel became identified with and ultimately burdened by the famous braided suit. What is there to identify absolutely Lagerfeld's style, except an ethereal lightness to his cut and flashes of wit?

Karl Lagerfeld does not expect to be judged on his past creations. Part of his pathological refusal to settle or identify comes out in his attitude to his own archives. He keeps nothing,

■ *Left: Chloé, spring/summer.*
Above: Chloé, autumn/winter.
Right: Chloé, spring/summer

to have an enclosed and private world. "I feel I belong to nowhere," he says. "I am German, but not from Germany as it exists today. My father was Swedish, my sister lives in America. I am most at home in Italy. My work is my life." If he is rootless, it must be because he chooses a

nomadic role, just as he chooses not to promote himself. He agreed to use the initials K.L. and a drawing of himself, complete with famous pony tail in silhouette for his latest perfume – only because the original name "Fanatic" was thrown out by the lawyers in a copyright confusion.

He has been the designer at Chloé for 20 years and has never sought to bring his own name to the forefront. "I like the idea of a lot of labels," he

nothing, nothing of his past work – never a favourite garment; not one single sketch. Carla Fendi has surreptitiously filed away the fruits of two decades of working together. But Karl would never consent to a retrospective of his work. (I can imagine his explosive reaction when he heard of the homage to Saint Laurent at the Metropolitan Museum in New York.) "To me the whole idea is horrible, against life," he says passionately. "I see people of my own age already looking back at the past. I never compete and never compare."

And yet this uncluttered personality keeps to the courtesies of the past. He never dictates to a secretary. He writes every single letter for business or pleasure by hand. Every note and detail and idea for his collection he writes down himself. (I hope someone is raiding the rubbish bins in the rue Cambon.)

He talks intelligently about his clothes, which tend to be of the British/Italian hybrid of cashmere and tweed, ever since he abandoned dressing up as an eighteenth century

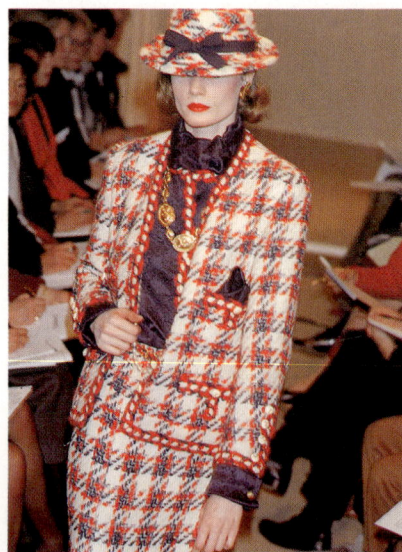

■ Left: Chloé, spring/summer. Above: Lagerfeld for Chanel couture collection, spring/summer. Right: Chloé, spring/summer

gentleman. In order to design the couture collection at Chanel, he steeped himself (some say foundered) in history, taking as his starting point the girlish, gay Chanel collection of 1939 (just before she closed her workrooms for 15 years).

He is not interested in intellectualising about fashion. I remember sitting in his salon fired by his fine claret (he doesn't drink) telling him that the French designers had beaten the Japanese threat by reviving the sexy/sexist look based on the classic Parisian principles of cut and chic.

"Have they won?" he asked me quizzically. "They are destroying half of fashion with this post-Hiroshima look. It is dangerous what they are doing. They are gambling with a kind of imbalance. I like to see what they do. The only thing I can't forgive the Japanese for, is that they have no sense of humour!"

And there, in his next Fendi collection, was the witty interpretation of the anarchistic influences from Japan (and from London designers whom he generously credited for their part in his inspiration).

Here were asymmetric coats with one sleeve cut out of balance with the other. There were odd marriages of fabric and raggedly cut skins. Big swathes of fur were wrapped across the body out of all proportion and dyed into the thunderous threatening grey palette of the Japanese designers.

Then the fashion computer fed in a different floppy disc and came up with skinny sexy suedes, elegant glossy furs, rich strong colours, all cut to the body with the utmost grace and style.

Karl Lagerfeld can tune into a fashion mood so perfectly that it is hard to believe with every collection that this is not his own definitive and personal fashion statement. As the cheers and bravos ring out, will the real Karl Lagerfeld ever stand up?●

SWEATS

GETTING PRETTY

● *By Sheridan McCoid*

Fashion has always borrowed and cribbed ideas from the sports field, but rarely so enthusiastically as during the last couple of years when we've seen the track suit walk off the running track on to the streets hand in hand with dance and exercise wear - looks now firmly established and fitting perfectly with today's more casual attitudes to dress.

And with its finger always firmly on the financial pulse, it's not surprising that America has had a lot to do with it all. As with all things American, when jogging and keep-fit became the trendy thing to do, it wasn't tackled by half and although losing all those inches and adding years to one's life were important, it somehow helped on those damp, chilly mornings tramping around Central Park, to be wearing the right gear. Enterprising designers were sitting atop a potential gold mine and the born-again track suit swiftly saturates the market with *de rigueur* discreet designer logos on collars and pocket being the make or break of a true jogger.

Fortunately, whether by coincidence, but more than likely by design, the right person picked up on sweatshirting as a fabric far too marketable to be relegated only to the keep-fit fanatic. Norma Kamali, innovative American designer, introduced her wonderful range of 'Sweats' which had little to do with running and everything to do with high-fashion. The ra-ra skirt, a snappy, gathered mini based on the cheerleader skirt, became her trade mark, as did those huge, cleverly cut sweatshirts with enormous shoulders.

The imitators were hot on her heels and soon, any girl that was worth her salt from seven to twenty seven, possessed at least one ra-ra. It was functional and often cheap. Old sweatshirts were dragged from the back of wardrobes, sleeves and

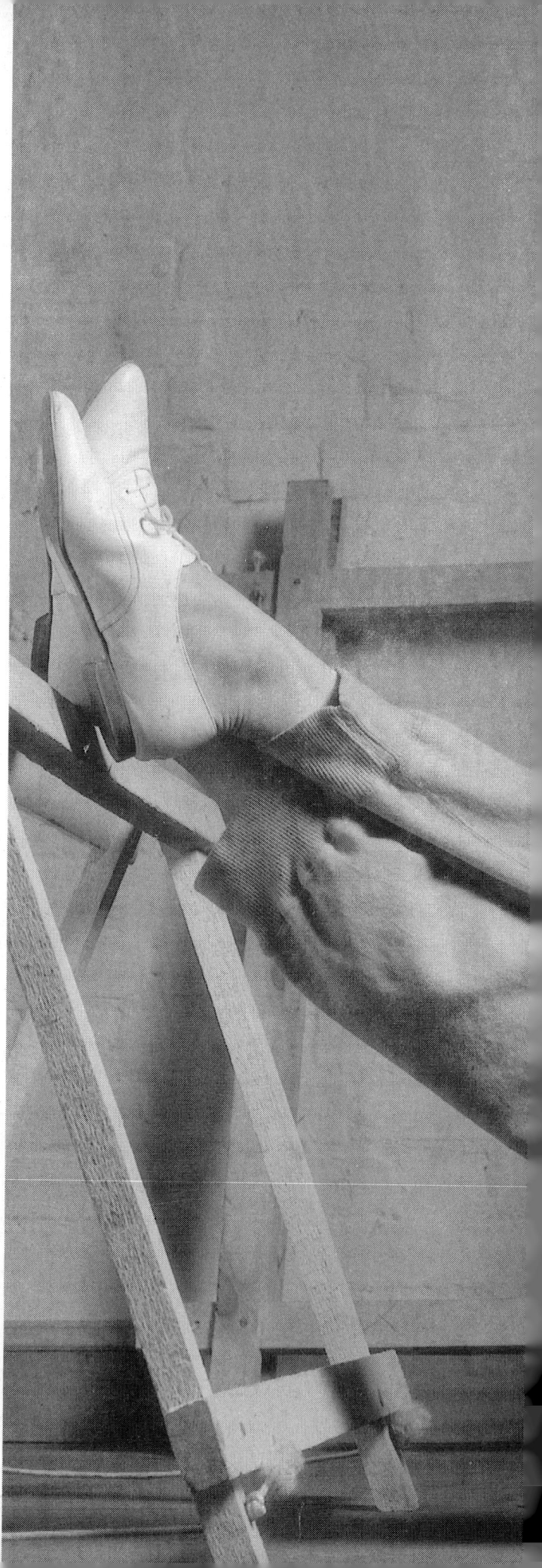

necklines carefully hacked off and if you didn't like what was written on the front, you simply turned the whole thing inside out.

Shortly after this came the dance boom with classes mushrooming almost overnight wherever there was room for half a dozen people to swing an arm and a leg. Jogging, after all, was a boring and lonesome pursuit and dance classes at places like the Pineapple Studio and the Dance Centre in London were filled to capacity from seven in the morning till late at night. And again, it all seemed much less painful to limber up in a well co-ordinated kit. Plenty of glamorous names helped to push this flourishing industry and it could have hoped for no greater clout than that given by Jane Fonda, exuding health from every pore, expounding on the benefits of aerobics. Big business raised its speculative head and dance wear switched from the barre to high-fashion.

With the exercise boom still going strong, looking set to last well into the eighties, there was plenty to inspire designers back to the sketch pad for this summer's crop of Sweats. The look has evolved into a

■ *Exercise-conscious summer sweats from the boutiques and chain stores brought a new, relaxed prettiness to holiday wear*

crisp, predominantly pastel blend of sports sweats and the more sexy, feminine touches of dance wear.

Jeff Banks, whose bright design sense has thrown the Warehouse chain of shops into the forefront of the young fashion market, says that every decade has a particular look that embraces the spirit of that period. "The eighties feel," he said, "is of great individuality coupled with sensible thriftiness." His range of pretty pastel skirts, cropped trousers, sleeveless cardigans and tops in sweatshirting were walking out of the shops long before summer had shifted into gear. Kamali's range for summer '83 was still full of her distinctive shapes with fabrics and colours that are peculiar to her only. Jumpsuits, shorts and draw-string skirts in fleecy pastels, white and grey; thermal cotton dresses, vests and skirts in pink, navy and white; a denim collection of shorts, tops and skirts and a resort range in lightweight cotton jersey.

Colours, small details and accessories were important. Grey was still popular, but stonewashed and overdyed in various pastel shades to great effect. Necklines, armholes and even hemlines were uneven and loosely overlooked; loose vests and tops were wide and often cropped to midriff length. Ballet pumps were still popular but so this summer were white canvas gym shoes and black or white canvas baseball boots. Enormous waistbands were cinched in with wide leather belts and lengths of fabric, which were also put to use knotted messily into the hair. Cotton leg warmers and fall-down socks flopped rather than sat neatly round the ankle. And bags were roomy and built for slinging over the shoulder. A simple and comfortable look, warmed up with thermals and layered, Sweats are perfect winter wear - both on and off the track. ●

■ *Chain-store ra-ra after Kamali*

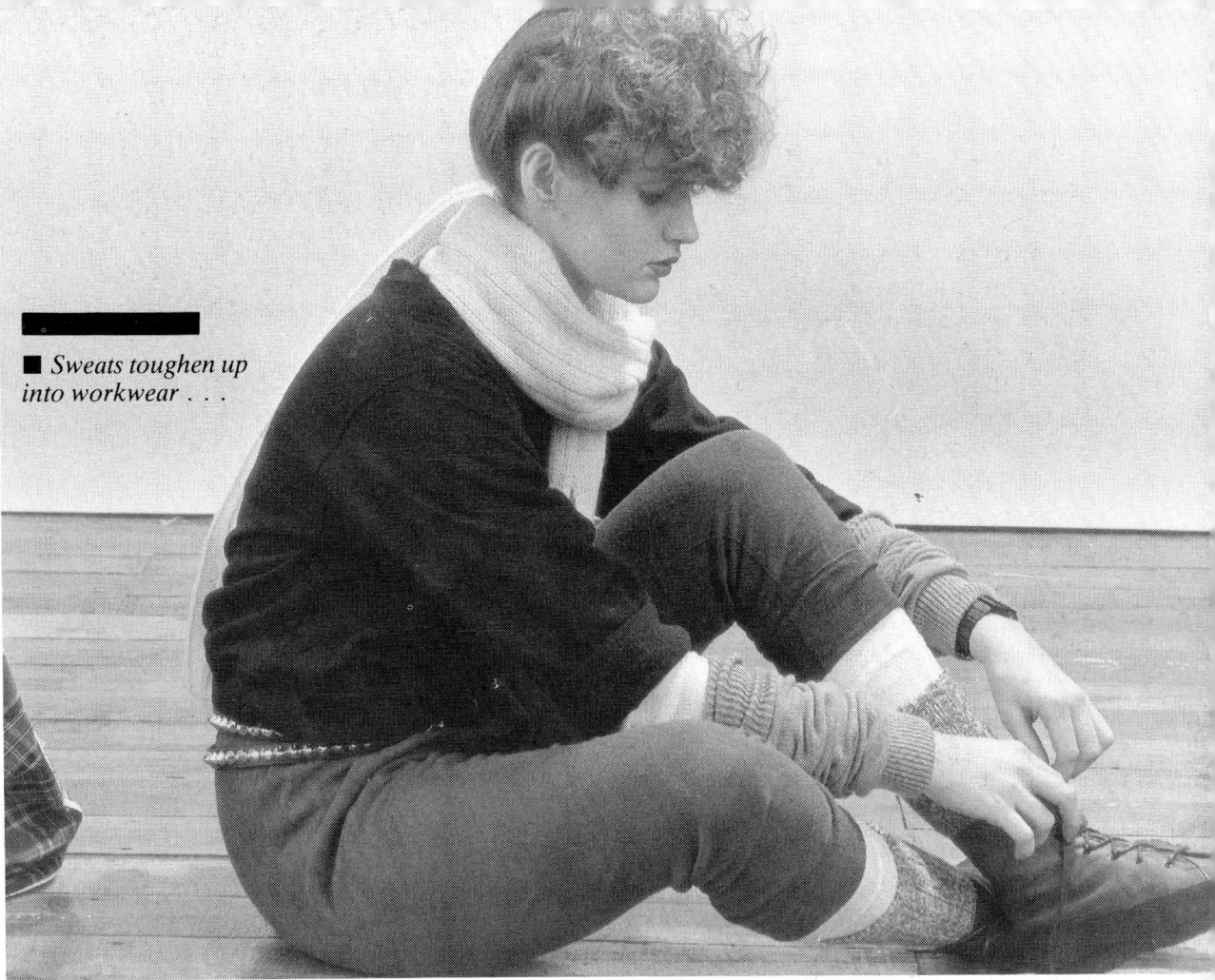

■ *Sweats toughen up into workwear . . .*

. . . and soften into Kamali's eveningwear

LACE

IN ROUGH COMPANY

● *By Brenda Polan*

There should be, close to the corner where Flood Street, Chelsea meets the King's Road and Antiquarius stands, a small shrine dedicated to Adam Ant, rock star. For before his particular version of the Romantic Revival sent dedicated followers of fashion into velvet breeches, brocade waistcoats and lots and lots of lace, Antiquarius was doing quite nicely selling none too costly antiques, bits of jewellery and second-hand clothes.

Its customers were mostly tourists and those metropolitan eccentrics who would kill for a genuine 1920s sequinned jacket. But in the winter of 1981-2 that all changed and lace became Antiquarius's runaway best-seller. Suddenly women were emulating their great grandmothers, busily accumulating bits of Needlepoint, pieces of Honiton, fragments of Brussels which they learned to use with the ingenuity of that earlier generation.

And the lace really did have to be old; if it wasn't, if it was nasty crisp white modern stuff, then they dipped it in cold tea to age it. Even in Mrs Gaskell's *North and South*, age has an added value. "Mrs Hale was .. . . captivated by some real old lace which Mrs Thornton wore"; "lace," as she afterwards observed to Dixon, "of that old English point which has not been made for this 70 years, and which cannot be bought. It must have been an heir-loom, and shows that she had ancestors."

The lace worn today proves nothing of the kind. It just proves that someone somewhere had careful ancestors, careful enough to wrap their lace in tissue, probably with a sprig of lavender, and put it away where the auctioneers would stumble unappreciatively across it a century later.

Adam Ant, of course, did not revive lace single-handedly. He merely produced its instant popularisation among the very young. The move

■ *Fragile antique lace with coarse-textured linens; a softening of the severe, voluminous shapes decreed by Japanese and British designers for spring*

towards Romanticism in dress was a logical development given the austere, even brutal styles which had preceded it. The true depths to be plumbed by the recession were just beginning to be appreciated and a depressed economy usually produces fantasy fashion.

In the USA Ralph Lauren, perhaps America's greatest ever stylist, produced a collection to which the name 'prairie' was appended. It was one of those rare fashion shows at the end of which the audience is on its feet stamping and yelling, the tears of sheer pleasure rolling down its collective cheeks.

The central theme was a sort of pioneer look: long flounced skirts often in suede or leather, plaid shirts, Fair Isle knitwear and lace fichus at the neck. It was a theme he was to develop through several seasons and it was one of the most copied looks in the history of fashion. But in October last year when he showed his collection for spring and summer 1983, even Lauren abandoned the nostalgia of his early American look for a much plainer American-modern style of dress.

The great advantage of romanticism in dress to designers is that the public loves it and embraces it wholeheartedly; the great disadvantage is that, when the designer wants to move on to, say, classic chic, the public wants to stay with romanticism. Which is what happened in this case.

Totally without the permission of any of the top designers, women were to be seen using their scraps of Nottingham to soften the severe shapes and rough textures decreed for spring and summer. It should not, given the way the clothes were shown on the catwalk, have worked, but it did. Firstly it worked because the rich texture of the lace complemented the equally rich but

■ *The old lending class to the new*

■ *Whether she bought it from Ralph Lauren, bid for it at an auction or inherited it from her grandmother, the 1980s lace-collector cherishes her pieces of Nottingham or Honiton and works them hard*

81

homespun sackcloth type textures of the clothes: sand, taupe, beige, dun, terracotta, greige and grey, white and cream and black. And thirdly it worked in exactly the same way it had worked with Ralph Lauren's plaid work shirts: because of its unexpectedness.

Having discovered how well bits of lace worked with the severe, volume-conscious clothes of spring, women explored the possibilities further and Antiquarius discovered that its unfussy Edwardian lace tops were in demand not as evening wear but to be worn under a bulky hopsack jacket, bepocketed and drooping at the hem and above newly revived baggy trousers.

There was suddenly a demand, too, for broderie anglaise to lighten and soften the crispness of the tailored jackets and skirts. Fashion designers and mass-manufacturers had not used broderie anglaise for spring '83 so it was back to Antiquarius and all its sister second-hand shops for peasant-style tops and prim little 1950s blouses.

Antiquarius's enormous success means that none of it is cheap. But that, it seems, is okay. The new generation of lace-wearers is happy to invest time and love in taking care of its lace. Just like great-grand-mother.●

HATS

● *By Brenda Polan*

"Nothing in nature or art", observed *Vogue* magazine round about 1930, "is so magically transforming as a wide drooping hat of summer lightness." The ability of hats to render the plain pretty and the unobtrusive quite dramatic is a theme to which the magazine has returned again and again over the decades. Of course, until the sixties changed all the sartorial rules, a lady was not considered dressed without her hat and gloves – from which she usually refused to be parted unless under her own roof.

But there is more to the hat business than mere old-fashioned decorum. If one's dress is a statement, one's headgear is its full stop – or, in some cases, its exclamation mark. A policeman, de-helmeted, has less authority; a meter maid without her aggressively peaked cap, starts to look like someone's girlfriend; a bishop without his mitre becomes just a balding old gentleman in a frock. Similarly, a vamp without her toque of feathers and diamanté is not really trying; an ingenue lacking her leghorn lacks also her charm; a grand dame without an imposing construction of satin, net, ribbon and a feathered corpse or two on her head just ain't that grand. A hat lends emphasis.

Except for occasions like weddings, barmitzvahs and royal garden parties where hats are *de rigueur*, headgear has had a poor time of it since Courrèges space helmet took millinery one giant stride into futurism and decline. Fashion was youthful, throwaway and the first bit to get thrown away was the hat – except when a comic, eccentric effect was sought. The seventies word was laid-back and hats, apart from crumpled baseball caps, didn't fit. Even the businessman's bowler has almost disappeared from the streets of London, its last bastion remains the ultra-traditionalist City.

There were other exceptions of course, some utilitarian, some symbolic. Jaunty yachting caps never lost popularity in certain sets; brightly coloured knitted pull-ons were used as emblems by Rastafarians; sheer necesssity turned a more chunky, less stylish kind of knitted hat into a membership badge for canvassers and campaigners; art school students have always understood the hat's potential for lending a bravura touch.

The majority started to catch on in the autumn of 1982 when young women began to sport felt trilbies, metal studded berets and mis-shapen, droopy brimmed hats inspired by Vivienne Westwood. Laid-back was laid–out; emphasis was back in style. When they showed their collections for spring and summer 1983, Europe's major designers showed they were in step. The abandoned jokey headdresses and floral wreaths in favour of proper hats: broad-brimmed elegant straws, net-trimmed fifties pillboxes, head-hugging, lavishly trimmed forties numbers which perched to the side, the front or the back but never sat square.

One factor in hats' new popularity was undoubtedly the way the young and dashing Princess of Wales looked in the ones she was forced, by her position, to wear. She is copied in all things irrespective of whether the copyists lead the same formal style of life or not. As David Shilling, London's *enfant terrible* of millinery (he was the terrible infant who used to make his mother, Gertrude, those ghastly giant headdresses in which she stole the show at Royal Ascot) commented: "In a matter of months she completely transformed young women's attitudes to hats. Suddenly you no longer had to be elderly or going to a wedding."

■ Broad-brimmed drama:
Frederick Fox

■ Perky straw:
Frederick Fox

Shilling is one of the most innovative milliners in London, the town where millinery has best survived its decline. His personal style is more than emphatic; it is almost theatrical and often positively baroque. That he is extending his talents into theatre design comes as no great surprise.

For him, spring 1983 was one of the best seasons he can remember. The same goes for Frederick Fox, milliner to, among others, the Queen. The Australian-born hatmaker reported: "March was the best month of my entire career in the business – and that's about 15 years. Sales were 100 per cent up on March 1982 and, most significantly, younger women seemed to have lost their inhibitions about hats. Certainly that is the part of the market I have consciously been developing".

"Monumental mum's hats are all very well and they will always be wanted for weddings, garden parties, the races, but there is much more fun in fashion, in designing hats which young women will find irresistible."

Young women in their thousands found Freddie Fox's simple lacquered straw with one perky matching feather irresistible. It was not an overpowering hat, nor a silly one. It was coquettish in an understated way. "I felt," said Frederick Fox, "that the mood for spring was a little Belle Epoque. That means hats that are quite high and sit on the head rather than pull down. But that doesn't mean you can't have quite a dramatic brim to peep from under."

Graham Smith, the young milliner who designs for collections like Jean Muir, hopes his own-label collection and designs for the mass-market hatmaker, Kangol, smiled a lot last spring, too. Like Frederick Fox, he explored the dramatic possibilities created by the graphic

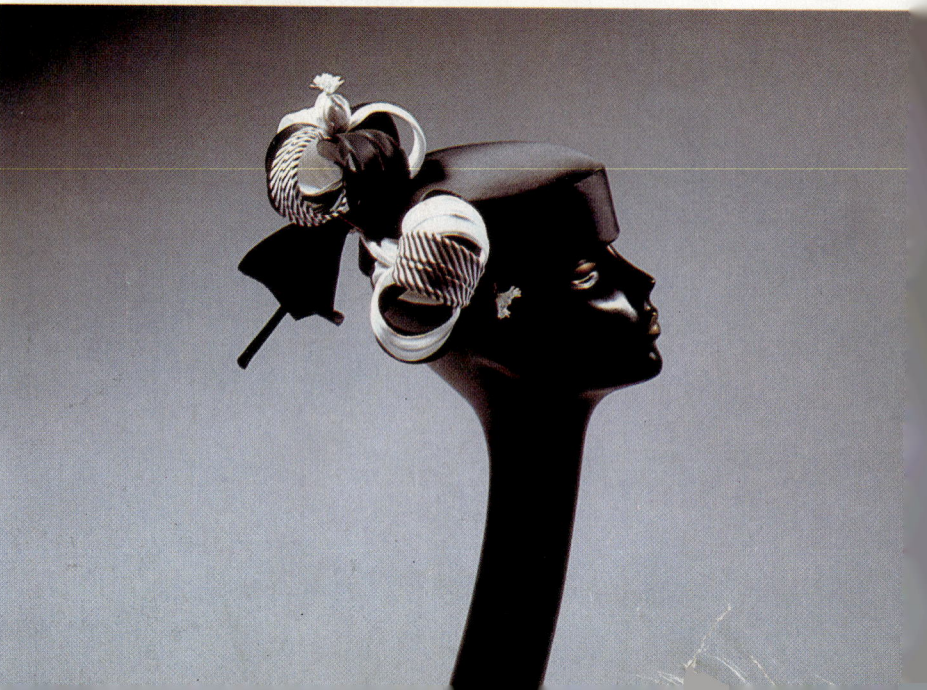

colours and strong, simple shapes of the clothes for spring and he responded to the romanticism of the soft pastels which came from the clothes designers, using silk flowers or net to soft-focus effect.

"It is," he said at the time, "a very hatty season. The wedding hat market changes little; that is a constant in a hatmaker's life. What has changed is the everyday hat market."

Change is probably too small a word. Resurrection is more like it; from a deathbed scene to success story almost overnight. "Well, there has always been the section of the market made up of the young and fashion-conscious who want something – like the studded beret I did for last winter – which is absolutely of the moment, has a certain amount of wit, a lot of style and does not cost much.

"The sudden development has been in the middle, between the wedding hat and the way-out hat, among the women who enjoy

■ *Clockwise from top left: cherry-laden skull cap by Frederick Fox; multicoloured abstract by David Shilling; Spanish hat by Graham Smith; lacquered straw with feather by Frederick Fox; decorated pillbox by David Shilling; monochrome simplicity by Alan Couldridge*

fashion but do not want to set it. For them it has suddenly become okay to wear a hat simply because it completes an outfit, it suits them and it is fun."

Down in Brixton, south of the Thames and miles from Mayfair millinery salons, much the same light-hearted mood prevails. The stylists on the streets of London have been completing their outfits with the right hat for several seasons and none are more hat-conscious than the young blacks of South London. The Big Apple, a hat-lover's heaven, is the shop where they get most of them. The owners, Dennis and Patricia White, import jaunty, raunchy, witty and simply sharply smart hats from America and Italy and sell them alongside equally amusing hats made in Britain.

Spring saw Dennis and Patricia conducting the last rites for the Rasta woolly pull-on and celebrating the rebirth of the panama-hatted dude. The Big Apple was joined by Demob, the Soho boutique, and other way-out-front shops in promoting Depression peaked caps, little felt pillboxes with clown

■ *Above: Masculine styled hats pirated by women. Right: Precarious fantasy by Steven Jones*

bobbles on top, trilbies, leather workingmen's caps and butcher boy giant berets.

As the clothes designers swung into winter at their March shows, the enthusiasm for hats was unabated. Autumn and winter being what they are weatherwise, however, the exuberance of the hats of spring and summer could not really be matched. A very hatty season indeed.●

SWIMWEAR

SLEEKER YET

● *By Brenda Polan*

The history of swimwear is a continuing tale of less and less. Sea bathing was not a fashionable activity until after the first world war; till then it was an unpleasant, medicinal activity prescribed by one's doctor for the alleviation of various conditions ranging from rheumatic twinges to insanity. Ladies for whom a series of dips was prescribed (it was a matter of immersion, not a paddle or a swim) would enter the water from the bathing machine, a modesty-preserving hut on wheels, clad in long drawers, flannel frock, girdle, bonnet and laced-up beach shoes. As the ad had it: you've come a long way, baby.

The furthest baby was to go was the topless swimsuit introduced in the mid-seventies by an otherwise obscure Californian designer, Rudi Gernreich. On beaches throughout the world toplessness survives but it has little to do with the self-conscious topless or one-breasted swimsuits which are still shown on the runways of the top designers. Nowadays baby just abandons her bikini top.

In fact, swimsuits are nearly always an embarrassment on the catwalk – which is surprising since today's fashion shows tend to be more exciting and sexier than the average high-price cabaret show. Somehow, a swimsuit beneath arc lights rather than the sun looks slightly indecent – especially a bikini.

It is hard to remember just how much of a fuss the first bikinis caused back in the late 1950s when almost Victorian attitudes to the body and its disclosure were common. The general acceptance of women in two tiny strips of cloth disporting themselves on the sea shore had a lot to do with the shift of emphasis from sea-bathing to sun-bathing.

A sun tan used to be something a lady simply

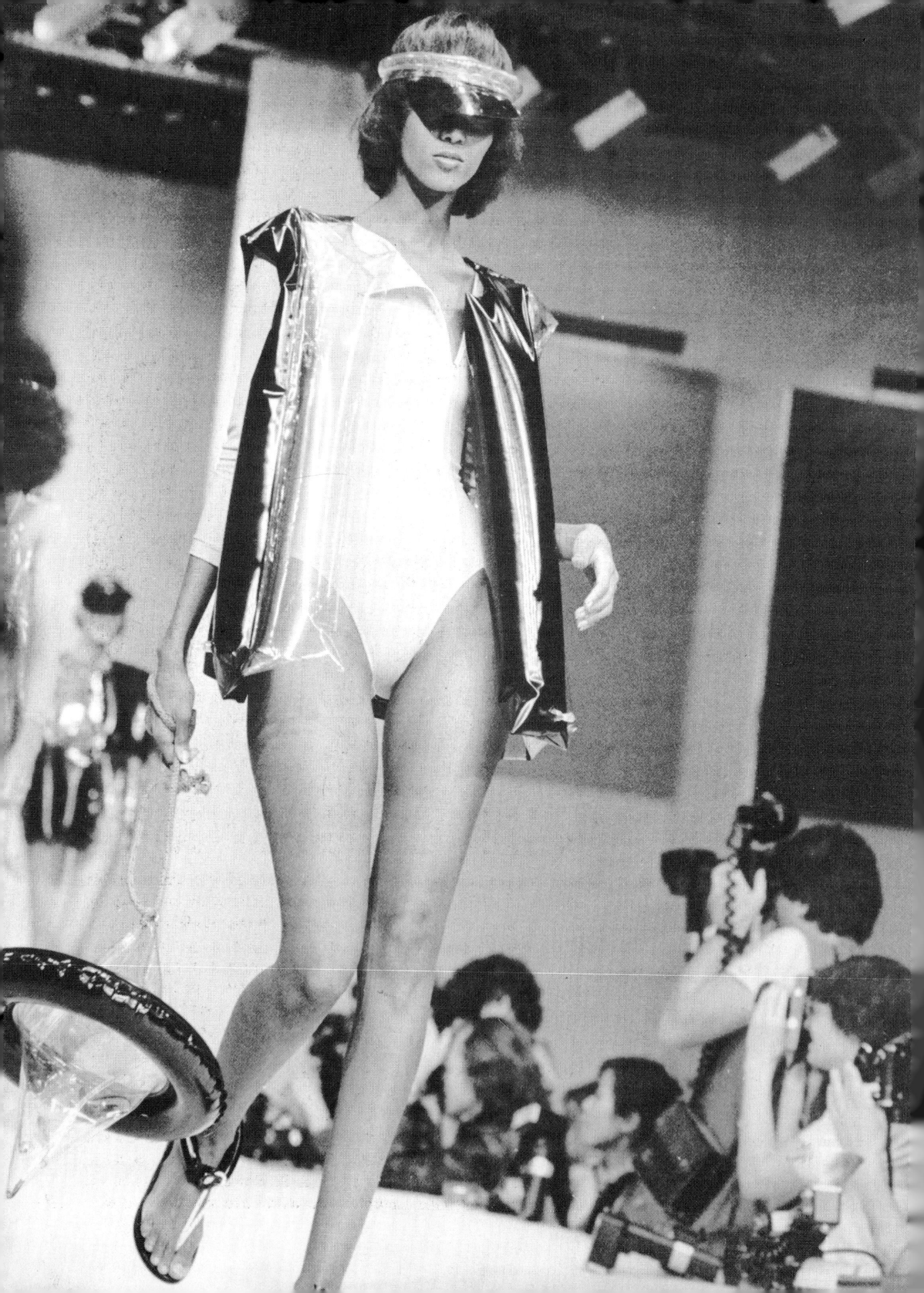

didn't get. It took the 1920s, the jazz age and the fashionable rich (many, until the Wall Street crash, American) summering in the South of France to appreciate the attractiveness of a tan.

And because Coco Chanel was a member of the Côte d'Azur set, brown was beautiful. It is of course, just a short step from what is fashionable among the rich to what is a status symbol among the not so rich. In this case a world war intervened to slow down the process, but, once Europeans were free once more to travel to the sunshine, they emulated their glamorous new world cousins and worked up a tan.

The bikini and eventual toplessness were inevitable simply because swimsuits, as the song made clear, were no longer primarily for swimming in; they were for tanning the skin in – and the greater the area of skin a woman could get tanned, the happier she was. There were summers, during the last two decades, when it was almost impossible to buy a one-piece swimsuit.

That was changed, as the eighties dawned, by a new body-consciousness. The shade of brown was no longer as important as a healthy-looking leanness, the result of jogging, exercise classes and, yes, swimming. Bikinis are not always easy to swim in; folklore abounds with tales of lost bikini tops and girls who can't come out of the water because of them. It might, of course, have been a matter of wishful thinking elaborating on one apocryphal incident – but women interested in twenty serious lengths of the pool preferred a one-piece.

A one-piece is sleeker, too, and reminiscent of the leotard in which aerobic heroines like Jane Fonda are almost always seen these days. So the designers of swimsuits (the best are Italian, Californian and

■ Left: Zippered and sporty on the Milan catwalk. Above: The vest as swimsuit

Israeli) for the summer of 1983 concentrated on a sporty look. True, they elaborated on the basic dance-class shape by using panels of colour or sewing on sequins, adding a frill here or a touch of ruching there, but their inspiration was easy to identify.

Fabric developments gave the designer's imagination more room for manoeuvre, too. Instead of corset-like garments made entirely of elastomane fibres, they were able to make only gently body-hugging garments whose resilience was provided by just 10 per cent Lycra mixed in with cotton or polyester. It made for greater comfort, a factor to which women had become accustomed in their everyday clothes and therefore demanded in their swimwear.

But although women enjoyed the one-piece for swimming, they remained true to the bikini for sun bathing. The desire to go home from St Tropez, Kos or Jamaica with a brown tummy dies hard. ●

■ *Opposite: Clockwise from top left: the frou frou suit; Gideon Oberson's sequinned glitz; fifties style in eighties fabric; Issey Miyake's gold and bronze warrior suit; the leotard as swimsuit. This page: A strange suntan but a sleek suit*

DIANA

PRINCESS SUPERSTAR

● *By Jackie Modlinger*

She's the world's most famous, most-photographed cover girl. Last year, Woman magazine awarded her the title of 'most elegant woman of the year in Great Britain'. That's Diana, Princess of Wales, Superstar.

Any young woman who can achieve such recognition and popularity in a scant two years could hardly fail to assert a major influence in her field. And, where fashion and beauty are concerned, the Princess of Wales excels.

Like her dashing predecessor and great-uncle-in-law, the Duke of Windsor, who launched the Windsor Cap and Windsor Knot, Diana, Princess of Wales has established herself as a fashion leader, whose presence has proved magical for the British fashion industry, both at home and abroad. Were the fashion industry to appoint a Patron Saint, the Princess of Wales would undoubtedly win the title.

Young and fresh, Lady Diana Spencer brought with her to her new role both spirit and enthusiasm. She resuscitated an ailing British fashion industry, generating the kind of excitement the country had lacked since the sixties. At a time when the British fashion trade was plunged into a bitter recession, the girl destined to be Queen single-handedly revitalized it, with a kick in the solar plexus that lifted us out of the doldrums and into international headlines. The Princess of Wales became Britain's best ambassadress and first lady of fashion.

There is no denying that, over the past two years, Diana has greatly influenced the way we dress. Her fashion diet spawned insatiable demands. A flashback to her (fashion) firsts calls to mind those looks she has launched and loved - from the top of her much-copied, fringed, sun-streaked bob, right down to those flat pumps, the salvation of shoe manufacturers, Clarks; from SuperSloane to Superstar, our Princess has proved a trailblazer all the way, and, endearingly, this has happened because of what she is, rather than who she is. The fashion industry has charted her progress, been a dedicated follower of her fashion taste and capitalized on it.

Fashion *per se* may not have supplied a directional look or trend, but the Princess has. The narrowing of class barriers, coupled with fashion's general diminishing direction, and, the fact that the Princess of Wales is a populist princess have combined to make her a fashion heroine.

In the Eighties, there are fewer real stars and those there are tend to reject glamour in their personal style. Love it or hate it, the Princess of Wales has a strong, eye-catching style, and, in a multi-faceted fashion world, single-mindedness is exemplary.

Charting her course from mere SuperSloane (well bred, well heeled upper class girl given to haunting Knightsbridge) to Superstar, the rag trade has followed her progress and hitched its wagon to this favourite Royal all the way.

Even when she was a mere Regulation Ranger (sharing a flat, working in a kindergarten) and still only Lady Diana Spencer, she had only to be photographed in a Laura Ashley piefrilled blouse with a sliver of velvet ribbon at the neck, a Peruvian sweater, a Loden coat, jeans, sneakers or knickerbockers, to create an unprecedented demand, an avalanche of orders. What she wore, the public wanted.

The first real sign, however, that Diana was destined to be an international fashion leader was that big black taffeta evening dress with its daring décolleté which she wore immediately after her engagement was announced to Goldsmith's Hall. Designed by David and Elizabeth Emanuel, this

■ *The Princess of Wales: her distinctive style has changed the face of fashion*

Diana has also lent weight to the jewellery business. Costume jewellery makers, Adrien Mann are on record as saying: "It is because of the Princess that pearl designs are selling well countrywide."

From the start Princess Diana surrounded herself with her own little coterie of designers. Virtually unknowns were catapulted into the limelight, thanks to HRH. One was

To the Court of Princess Diana, and helped in no small way by Anna Harvey, a Senior Fashion Editor on the British edition of Vogue magazine, came other designers whom the Princess continues to patronise, occasionally widening the net.

Diana has been heavily criticised on account of the considerable amounts she is reputed to spend on

was the dress that triggered off a whole romantic revival and launched a million look-alikes. Thanks to the Princess, the big taffeta ballgown was to rustle for a further 18 months, and foreign store buyers began once again to look to Britain for what she does best - big evening dresses.

1981 was declared, thanks to Di, the Year of the Hat, and as it progressed, Diana created a demand for the Blouse Beautiful - white Victorian blouses were suddenly snapped up. Lyn Morris, Senior Selector for the Ladies Blouse Department at Marks and Spencer recalls: "As soon as Diana did that engagement picture, our fastest-selling style was a side-tying Lady Di blouse." The Marks & Sparks version sold for £9.99. The fashion industry followed Diana's every footstep avidly, aping her appetite for sumptuous fabrics like silk, satin, velvet and lace. Likewise, her fondness for antique lace collars worn with cameo pins on velvet dresses started a trend which has yet to fade.

■ *Left: The perfect Princess complete with ribbons and pearls. This page: two of her many, stunning hats and another version of the one-shoulder dress*

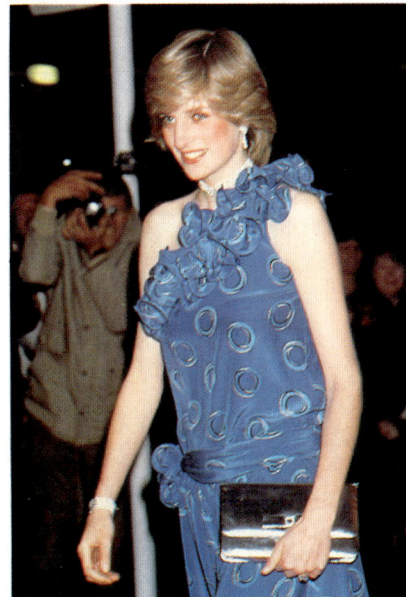

'Battersea Bill' Pashley, alias 'Mr. Frantic Frocks' who made the tailored checked tweed blouson suit the Princess of Wales wore for her honeymoon photocall at Balmoral.

her royal wardrobe, ostensibly in the region of some £1,000 a week, £70,000 a year. But what has to be weighed up is that the operation is in fact cost-effective, for the spin-offs for the British fashion industry are far-reaching and tip the balance in her favour. She can, it might well be argued, be forgiven her indulgences, for she is a fashion patriot.

Nevertheless, it is estimated that in a year the Princess of Wales may order as many as 200 dresses or suits, 50 evening dresses and coats and almost 300 hats. Can any woman, speculate her critics, need so many clothes? Of course, unlike her mother-in-law, Diana takes enormous pleasure in her clothes, enjoying choosing them, giggling happily at the endless fittings and consultations and responding with wide smiles when the public oohs and aahs at her latest outfit.

And the makers of all those clothes benefit enormously. Take, for example, that celebrated sheep sweater, designed by Warm & Wonderful. Just how has it affected the business of partners, Joanna Osborne and Sally Muir? Reports Joanna: "All I can say is that it has really helped our business, especially with the particular jumper in question....it has greatly increased our trade....in fact it is still selling, although the Princess wore it before she got married....we are trying hard to do other things, but we can't get away from the sheep sweater." So there you go. Dyed in the wool. We're just a herd of sheep where the Princess of Wales is concerned.

Designers like Bellville-Sassoon, Caroline Charles, Jasper Conran, Bruce Oldfield and Gina Fratini have been patronised by the Princess of Wales and continue to be firm favourites. The Emanuels and David Neill and Julia Fortescue, who were among her earlier

choices, seem to be out of favour, though Lady-in-Waiting Anne Beckwith Smith had an outfit for the Australian tour from the latter.

If anyone thought that impending motherhood would remove the Princess from the fashion stakes, they were wrong. The pregnant Princess has done more for maternity fashions than any other mother-to-be. Before the royal pregnancy, whoever had heard of

Charles Design? She taught other would-be mums to distract attention from the bulge and showed the way: collar it white, collar it light, with lace against the face, was the new maternity message.

The entire nation felt for her when she made her first public post-William appearance for the Falklands Thanksgiving Service. Like all new mothers, she hadn't quite regained her waist. But shortly Diana was to prove the point that a woman can never be too rich or too thin. A Gala Fashion Spectacular in aid of Birthright saw her slimmed

down to model size, so much so that in the popular press speculation raged as to whether or not the girl was anorexic.

That was the night the Princess of Wales changed the tone of evening-dressing, declaring the big taffeta ball gown dead. A bright blue medallion-spotted one-shouldered chiffon confection, sleek and pared-down in shape, eclipsed the big ballgown in a night's work. The designer behind her new svelte look was Bruce Oldfield, who says: "I think that she's become the current most watchable woman in the world and the fact that she's British and wears British clothes can do nothing but good. The one-shouldered dress

girl would wear junk. She's made that look new again; she's put fun into a look of fashion establishment things."

Another designer whose clothes she chooses is Caroline Charles. "She's very interested in clothes and also very humorous about them, both good reasons why she should continue to both influence and set trends," she says. "Nobody who is photographed continually has as much influence. Other people aren't aped - take Elizabeth Taylor, for example. The Princess of Wales's clothes suit most women, so she becomes a Princess of the people. Her fashions are easy, pretty clothes with which women can identify."

Royal milliner, John Boyd, enthuses about his 'Wee Lassie' as he affectionately dubs the Princess: "Her influence is enormous and I think she will continue to set trends;

for the Guildhall? I was very pleased when the Princess chose something out of keeping with her normal style. I think she looked splendid.

"She's tall, has the kind of figure every girl would want. The big ballgown is slightly obsolete; it was right at the time for the traditional, romantic look of the wedding, but now we're back to long, sleek, slinky looks."

■ *The distinctive style of the Princess is obvious from casual daywear through to velvet evening gowns*

Whatever Diana wears, the rest of us get offered, albeit most reasonably reproduced. Within a few days, the Peter Robinson store had a similar one-shouldered evening dress in their Oxford Circus windows.

One of her favourite designers, David Sassoon, says of HRH: "I think that she has had a tremendous influence. She has revitalised the industry - she has made fashion a status thing, but stylishly. Take, for instance, the way she wears jewellery - she wears the real thing, but in that same throwaway way a young

after all, she's the only one. She has several different types of hats coming up. Some are a wee bit bigger, with the brims lifting, not so straight or drooped. She's had a bright pink sailor hat, and this seems to be one of her favourite colours. She has several hats in that strong, pink colour, with slightly more blue in it. She's had the pillbox shape, and she's having a breton-style-hat with the brim rolling up fractionally."

One of Diana's newest protegées is Arabella (Bella, for short) Pollen, introduced through the Vogue network. The Princess of Wales seems to have a penchant for Bella's tweed coat-dresses with velvet collars and cuffs, and loved her summer sailor and Deauville looks. "I am sure she will continue to be an

■ *The going away outfit resurfaces in Australia and right, Diana charms the crowd in bright red*

influence on the fashion world, and I think that she has helped the industry in general," says the designer. Diplomacy is paramount where the Princess is concerned, for look what happened to the Emanuels. They cashed in too fast and too loudly on Royal patronage and, though their tights, sunglasses and bedlinen may be selling well, they have only just, two years later, been restored to favour.

They could take credit for the apricot taffeta ballgown she wore to the state dinner in Wellington, New Zealand, one of the many evening dresses which contributed so sub-

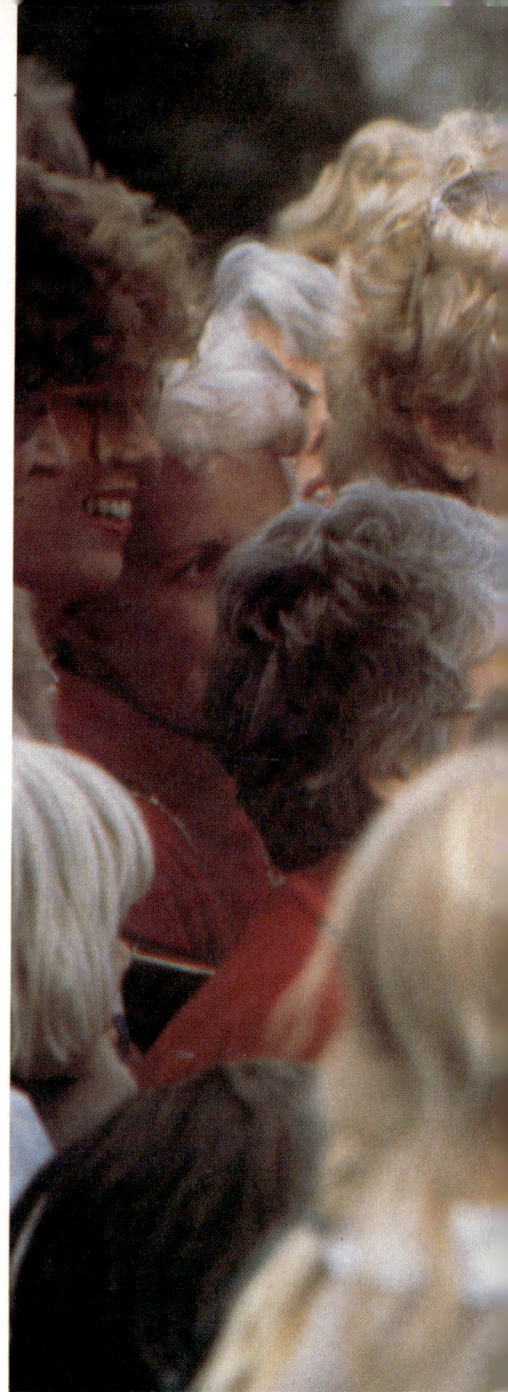

stantially to her astounding success on the royal tour down under.

Bruce Oldfield scored two hits: the first with his glittery blue organza ruffled evening dress worn to the ball at Sydney Opera House the night the Prince of Wales waltzed her off her feet; the second, a red and silver spangled ballgown with flounced neckline and hem, appeared at another state reception, this time in Hobart.

For the record, the Princess wore 50 outfits in 42 days, although not all of them were new. Her melon-coloured going-away outfit, her red

jerkin suit and the daisy-sprigged fuschia silk suit first worn at Prince William's christening (all by Bellville Sassoon) got a second outing. But as the tour progressed, British designers were scanning the newspapers and chalking up credits. Jan Vanvelden was the hot favourite. The princess chose to wear at least four of his outfits, often with serrated collars – even though the green spotted dress with elbow-length puffed sleeves worn for Prince William's "al fresco" photo-call, was on back to front.

Credit, too, to Benny Ong (the simple white embossed cotton dress that climbed Ayers Rock), to Donald Campbell whose fuschia/white spotted back-buttoning dress went to Fremantle Hospital, to Arabella Pollen whose coffee/cream striped two-piece was dubbed pyjamas by the none-too-knowledgable Aussies. They actually accused her of looking "dowdy, matronly, frumpy, skinny and not showing enough leg". But then, whenever has an Australian (except a few lone expatriates) been any kind of arbiter of taste?

Even they, however, had to concede they were enchanted by Hachi's bare-shouldered, white hand-beaded evening gown worn to a gala ball in Melbourne. They wanted a sexy Princess? They got her.

As for the Princess herself, she will continue to lead and to delight her public. Social Democratic Party President, Shirley Williams, is on record as predicting the shape of things to come for 1983: "Life will only be lighted," she prognosticated, "by the Princess of Wales adopting increasingly astonishing fashions." ●

PARIS

● *By Sally Brampton*

Whoever it was who said that fashion was a common, international language was speaking with forked tongue, or from an ordered age that is now but a memory. That any single, definitive look ever existed seemed impossible in the early sun that shone on Paris in the springtime of this year. At the unveiling of the autumn collections two opposing cultures, the French and the Japanese (a powerful influence with 11 of their designers showing there) met on the historic catwalks with a resounding clash, and proved that while the French speak a colourful and exuberant patois, the Japanese continue to communicate in their own mysterious way. There were more minor reverberations too, as successive designers set out to stamp their individual mark on a world that no longer heeds sartorial rules.

While it was surprising that the chauvinistic Parisians should allow the Japanese to invade their sacred ground, it came as no surprise at all that they should meet the onslaught with scarcely marked aggression. References to the "post-atomic look" and "intellectual bag ladies" did not go unnoticed, but it was the clothes themselves that graphically illustrated the differences in ideology. It was as if the radically new Japanese ideas forced the Parisian designers to become more French that the French themselves. They answered the sombre oriental statement with suitably Gallic colour and more than one scornful swish of a well rounded derrière. The jokes were as elaborate as the shows themselves, and in many cases as lacking in subtlety. The fashion victim's newest hero, Jean Paul Gaultier, opened his show with a kimono clad creature who did the bcount-foot shuffle up the catwalk to the chink chink of chopstick music. The

audience cared not one whit that he had got his cultural wires crossed; they were simply delighted to be allowed to share a joke after a couple of days spent puzzling over the Japanese designer's influential but essentially humourless ideas.

It was a landmark, that spring in Paris. Not since the sixties has there been a movement strong enough to threaten the very fabric of established fashion. The movement had been gathering strength for some two years by then, but it was the first time the Japanese had put on a show of such strength. In fact the designers were merely the catalytic fuel on the fire that had been blazing since the Japanese group, Itokin, announced the purchase of 50 per cent of the shares of the couture house of Courrèges.

However, there is nothing like a direct threat to make the French take up their scissors and defend their reputation. When the eyes of the world averted its gaze to the distant shores of America, the Parisians got themselves off their well groomed and rather superior backsides and replied with a season that had the fashion press writing banner headlines proclaiming that "Paris was back on top". The ways in which the French designers reacted to the mystery of the Japanese presence (which one suspects may remain an eternal mystery to some) proved their maturity as designers.

Thierry Mugler, the one-time enfant terrible of Paris, but now quite grown-up – in years anyway – reacted with his usual wicked humour. His comic strip heroines became even more comic and certainly more stripped. There was no need for any man to undress Mugler's women with his eyes; their charms were abundantly on show, sleekly outlined in curve-cut velvet, tweed and corduroy suits. Mugler had already announced that he was looking for "fat models" as a reaction against those "skinny

THIERRY MUGLER

CLAUDE MONTANA

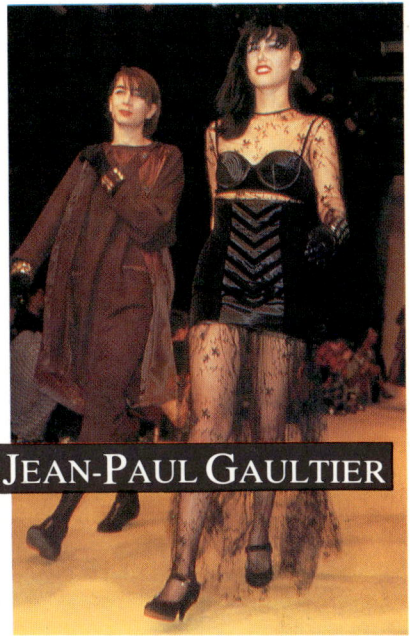

JEAN-PAUL GAULTIER

black clad existentialists" – whoever could he have meant? He seemed unable to find any so made up for it by transforming the reed slim mannequins into voluptuous sirens draped in Harlow jersey sheaths slung together by the merest wisp of diamante. They were an amazing feat of suspension which failed to suspend the imagination once the occupier of the gown shifted a millimetre. His finale, a splendid show of operatic blood red and passionate purple velvet gowns, was breathtaking; the audience simply gasped with relief when the star diva swooned to the floor clasping a poisoned cup in one languid hand.

While Mugler may lack subtlety, he has never lacked the ability to produce the kind of overtly sexual clothes that keep his audience in raptures and him in millions. He found his formula and has stuck to it for some time – and well he might until someone comes along who can do it better. Someone did. Azzedine Alaia is the new sex symbol of Paris. He succeeded, without fanfares or five mile long catwalks in forcing the major buyers and journalists to beat a path to his tiny showroom door. Beating down the door was even

KENZO

more difficult, although many tried it. His clothes are quite simply, sensationally sexy, but his cut is so clever, his fabrics so rich and his tailoring so artful that any intimations of vulgarity are dispelled. He makes women look like women, and unlike some male designers understands where a woman's curves naturally lie and where nature can be discreetly improved upon.

His hour glass dresses, sculpted in wool or suede were worn with short swinging sheepskin jackets or enormous double-breasted coats that narrowed from wide coat hanger shoulders to exaggerate sensuously slim hips.

This emphatic V-shaped silhouette was rampant throughout Paris, but nowhere more so than at Claude Montana – the acknowledged king of exaggerated form. His leathers and suedes, which are generally good, were triumphant. He first popularised the strong shouldered jacket shape which curves to a low hip and he again proved that nobody does it better. He had left the short, snappy skirts of spring far behind but swept fabric into full form or long slim calf-hitting lengths.

UNGARO

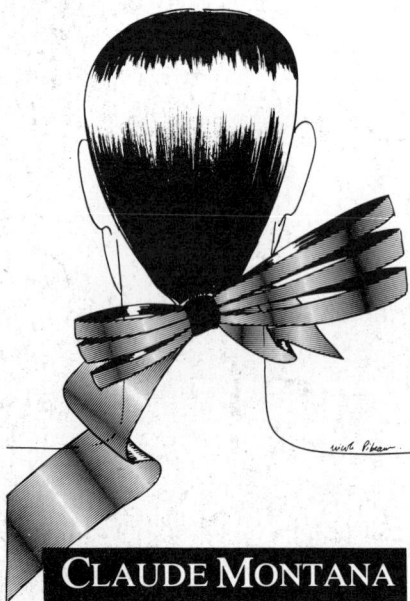

CLAUDE MONTANA

CLAUDE MONTANA

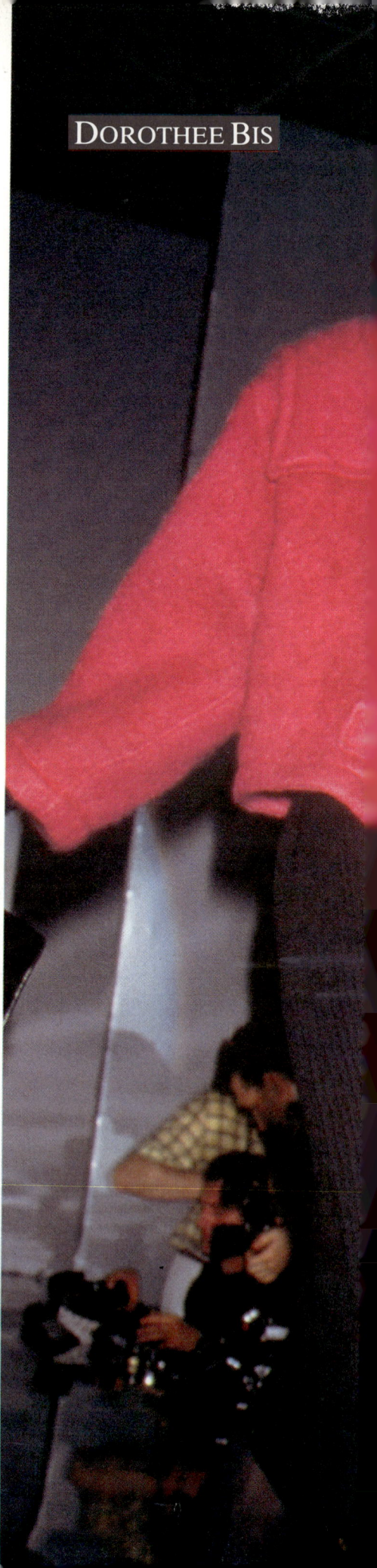

ANNE-MARIE BERETTA

DOROTHEE BIS

While Montana proved his rightful place as a leading talent, it was Karl Lagerfeld who more than any other designer distilled the essence of Paris and all that it represents as a leader of fashion. His collection for the house of Chloé was his best ever. He combined elegance with humour, and wearability with that magic ingredient that is so often missed by designers who aspire to produce 'wearable' clothes – style. His line was long and sensuous; drawn by the sparing hand of an instinctive designer. He swept knits over knits without making them look clumsy, lowered the revers of jackets and coats to waist level and

CHLOE

below without making them look absurd, and neatly side-stepped the length issue by showing double hems or long slim skirts that still had fluidity and movement. His slim, supple evening dresses flowed and sparkled like streams of water – literally; for he had embroidered taps and showers at the necks of columns of black silk that rained showers of diamonds to the hem.

Lagerfeld is a man of many talents. Not only did he design the brilliant Fendi fur collection but he also designs the Chanel couture collection and rumour has it that he has more than a little to do with the prêt-à-porter as well. Whether he masterminds it, or it is simply the

CHANEL

SONIA RYKIEL

CHANEL

CHANTAL THOMASS

spirit of his couture line that breathes life into it, it was a collection that did justice to the memory of the late, great Coco. The distinctive Chanel suit remains, slimmed down and revved up, as do the simple cashmere cardigans worn with torrents of gilt and pearls at the neck and wrists.

A classic style never dies, but it does sometimes petrify or, growing bored of itself attempt to slip off its immaculate lines and make new tangents. Sonia Rykiel, who has her classic formula well established, deviated from it with printed dresses that had apron fronts blooming like galleons in full sail. That was just the build up to her full frontal sweaters with which she paid tribute to her pregnant daughter, Nathalie. Private jokes are not made to be shared and few people appreciated the new silhouette. The remainder of the collection was vintage Rykiel, characterised by her customary snake-hipped silhouette softened by languid bows at the neck.

Sonia Rykiel is one of the main exponents of the matchless, polished elegance that is so par-

YVES ST LAURENT

ticularly French. That other great arbiter of style, Yves Saint Laurent, continued to show his disdain for 'le fashion' and kept well within the confines of 'le classic'. As he frequently does, he declared himself to be "beyond and outside fashion". He certainly went outside the general direction by showing trousers where all others concentrated on skirts. His essential look was based on the simple tunic, which appeared in all fabrics and lengths and while he shocked his devotees with a rather alarming use of colour – burnt orange and purple seemed to be a favourite combination – he reassured them by producing a group of immaculate black and white checked suits that bore his unmistakable handwriting. It was a well paced collection, but like all his prêt-à-porter shows it lacked the fire of his couture, for it is in his couture that he inevitably finds the freedom to make his strongest statements.

Kenzo's show also lacked fire, but one suspects that what was an excellent collection suffered the same fate as the gimmick-free Saint Laurent line, diminished as it was by the glaring spotlights of the now ridiculously elaborate catwalk shows, where the clothes take second place to the presentation. His collection was a judicious balance of all his best looks; there was little that was new, but Kenzo's youthful zest never ages. He layered jackets over jackets, swept kimono coats over long hip-belted tunics, sliced up skirts shorter than any in Paris, and mixed print and colour with his usual exuberant charm. Kenzo may be Japanese by birth, but he is purely Parisian by design. He has never had any problems with cultural contradictions and continues to span the chasm between Fashion West and Fashion East with extraordinary ease.●

KENZO

STILL LIFE BY
GIORGIO ARMANI

MILAN

RETURN TO CLASSICISM

● *By Brenda Polan*

Despite the fact that he chose, yet again, to show his clothes as a static display rather than on the runway, Armani once again dominated the Milan ready-to-wear shows held in early March. And although his relaxed exhibition should have paled next to the razzamatazz of the catwalk shows to follow, it didn't. Giorgio Armani had the clearest and loudest statement to make in Milan and, though many were initially disconcerted by it, it was heard.

He summed it up himself: "Fashion has been overdoing it. It has been trying too hard, over-indulging its ideas and producing clothes which threaten to swamp the personality of the wearer. The time has come for a return to basic concepts: purity and simplicity."

With varying degrees of commitment and success, the rest of the Milanese designers expressed the same thought. There was in Milan, as the designers showed their autumn/winter collections, a more low-key mood than in recent seasons. March's shows were shorter, less pretentious, more coherent; the clothes themselves were untricky, stylish, covetable; the people – sellers, buyers, reporters, observers – were, as a consequence, more confident and relaxed. And, to the amazement and bright-smiling pleasure of all concerned, the sun shone.

True, in the vast Fiera di Milano with its large show halls, its clutter of showrooms, restaurants, press rooms, magazine stalls, flower shops and bank, no one got to bask much in the sun, but just knowing it was there lifted the spirits. This was how Italy was supposed to be. And this, too, was how Italian clothes were supposed to be.

To call this a return to Italian classicism is a little too glib; it leaves out the sense of excitement which

119

was certainly there. But it was in keeping with that Milanese sense of style which makes Italy world leader in the fields of furniture and interior design. Its components are finely honed craftsmanship, an understanding of the need for discipline, an awareness of the modern world and the needs of the people who inhabit it, a playful imagination but no French *folie,* and a businesslike approach.

Although Armani showed his own-label collection as still life, the collections which he designs for Erreuno and Mario Valentino were held with all the usual hype, heat and hysteria on the runway. They were strictly in the same slightly softened geometric shapes – unadorned short tent dresses, almost severe little suits with short, collarless jackets and short straight skirts, some with dramatic slits to aid walking. Many jackets wrap over in front with that relaxed bloused effect which Armani has used through several seasons. Trousers, which were quite rare in this collection, were full length and comfortably wide in the leg, pleated into the waistband. Coats were long, classic in shape, generously cut.

And although the shapes and the amount of detailing varied richly from designer to designer, that held true throughout the shows. The Italians went for the clean spare look of collarless, box-shaped jackets or for the fluid, big-brush look of large, easy-to-pull-up-around-the-ears revers on generously cut blouson or enormous swinging coat. They are still playing with asymmetry too, which surely reached its ultimate and most graceful expression in Gianni Versace's flared short jacket with one triangular lapel ending mid-midriff and one long one, gradually widening till it reaches the jacket hem.

LUCIANO SOPRANI

GIANNI VERSACE

To vary the short pencil skirt, the Italians offered long circular or pleated skirts or the narrow 'longuette', reminiscent of suffragettes, which Luciano Soprani included in both his own-label and the Basile collections. Box-pleated or gently gathered at the waist or from a basque, the longuette gives a slender silhouette, stops just above the ankle, and can be side, front or back-buttoned. It will undoubtedly become beloved of all women who live in cold climates.

It is already beloved of most of the women who watched it down the runway. Both Soprani's collections were, in fact, greeted with rapture. A shy man in his early forties, Luciano Soprani only emerged fully from behind the Basile label two seasons ago when his own-name label was launched. But he has always had his fans – women who love his relaxed tailoring and his sensuous feeling for fabric and colour.

The Italians have a taste for sombre colours, used along with maybe white or cream or a splash of scarlet to dramatise it, or used together in unexpected juxtapositions, and Soprani is the master of this skill. He loves tobacco with black, light navy with taupe, and rich variations of beige, greige, grey, charcoal, mushroom and brown. Some of the fabrics he used are stolen straight from menswear; others, like his rich, almost monochrome plaids, Irish tweeds and softest gabardines are certainly womenswear fabrics but still manage to hint at the discretion of menswear.

From these fabrics he fashioned, for autumn, some superbly cut peg-topped wide pants, tulip-shaped long jackets and long, tapering tweed coats with wrap-around asymmetric collars. The fans – and the rest – got to their feet to

TOUCHE

GIANFRANCO FERRE

applaud. Their number included the actress, Jacqueline Bisset, nominated, in a surprisingly showbizzy gesture, Basile's woman of the year. Well, she is successful, she is rich, she is talented – and she is very independent and grown-up. The other qualities aside (although they fit the Soprani image) you do have to be rich and you do have to be grown up to wear Soprani.

Another Milanese star, Gianfranco Ferre, got himself a standing ovation. He has also returned to proper trousers after all those seasons of breeches, knicker-bockers and hacked-off pants. His

are front-pleated, roomy and beautifully tailored, worn with his dramatic blouson tops in patchwork suede and ribbed knit with deep raglan sleeves and asymmetric neck fastenings.

His classy beaver-lamb trimmed coats had raglan sleeves, too, and, although basically classic in cut, they were long, voluminous, swirling – definitely on-the-march coats. It was a coat which appeared again and again – at Soprani and Basile, at Krizia in greys and charcoals lifted with cream, at Complice where Claude Montana was faithful to his own feeling for hierarchic mass (or

intimidating bulk, if you prefer), at Missoni which produced a strongly proportioned classic collection in rich colour combinations, and at Byblos where the British designer, Keith Varty finished them off with enormous cape collars and wide, curved shoulders.

Sportmax is first and foremost a producer of superb coats and jackets and in this collection, by the Frenchman, Guy Paulin, they were especially strong, the sense of volume perfectly controlled in tweed or wool velour, sometimes trimmed with the beaver lamb which made an appearance in most

MISSONI

collections, Paulin, along with Varty and Montana, also allowed himself more than a fleeting nod in the direction of the fading fifties look with acid-coloured plaids and houndstooth checks. After four days of Italian sobriety, it looked terribly vulgar and not at all amusing.

Vulgarity crept into the Fendi collection, too, where Karl Lagerfeld tends to indulge his wildest fantasies (or darkest nightmares). Even the least sentimental must have felt the merest tremor of doubt when the unperturbed model with half a dozen whole mink corpses (heads, whiskers, claws and tails) fashioned into a headdress, tripped by. But the core of the collection, mostly furs, some suede and leather and Donegal tweed plus knitwear, gabardine tunics and stunning little black dresses, was masterly.

The show started with a raggedy Japanese-inspired look: shaggy, patchily dyed furs mixed with smooth in huge, abstract shapes, some with caveman panels floating or tossed cape-like over a shoulder – a style known as *sauvage* or Raquel Welch. As the long show progressed, the colours of the furs became ever more lyrical, leaving natural browns, tans, blacks and blond behind in favour of deep burgundy, peach, ice blue. The cut became less fantastical and more fabulous – a display of opulent beauty rare even in the world of high fashion, and in a mood all its own.

The emphasis on linearity and the drama of simplicity which pervaded the daywear clothes was to be seen in the eveningwear, too. Laura Biagiotti, whose design philosophy is based on her own experience as a working mother, has a light and magical touch with dresses – especially taffeta cocktail dresses. She is famous for her easy 'bambola'

LAURA BIAGIOTTI

GIANNI VERSACE

GIORGIO ARMANI
FOR ERREUNO

(doll) dresses which are basically tent-shaped but so cleverly flounced, pin-tucked, or otherwise detailed that the wearer can be chic while she is comfortable.

This season Biagiotti's tongue was well in her cheek as she elaborated her white taffeta choir-boy's surplice (high church and very pretty) into a vicar's nightmare in hellfire scarlet with overdone trimmings. Her cashmere shift dresses, however, which are another of her strengths, were severe tubes with scarf-shaped floating panels which tie at hip or shoulder – stunning to look at and a relaxed, modern way to dress.

Biagiotti's dressage look of grey flannel redingote, cream breeches, silk stock and riding boots, though somehow out of step with the rest of Milan, looked startlingly good – a traditional upper-class style of dress which always translates well from the paddock to the street. Another country-into-town style which works just as well came from Mariucca Mandelli at Krizia. This consisted of a classic tweedy long blazer over waistcoat and short, schoolgirlish box-pleated skirt.

Elsewhere Mandelli used country

127

MARIUCCA MANDELLI
FOR KRIZIA

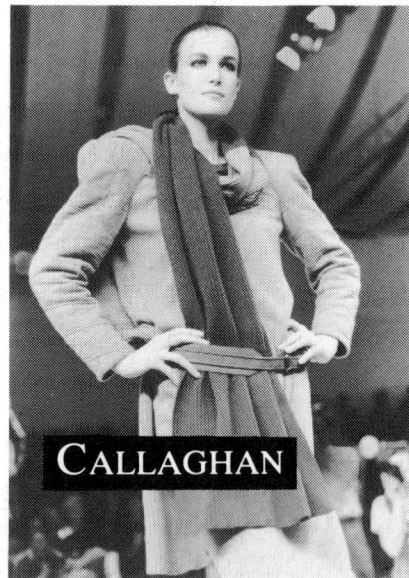

CALLAGHAN

ever, is Gianni Versace's feather-light chain mail which, this season, he embroidered and appliquéed for additional richness. These Greek-draped, wonderfully fluid tops in rich, burnished metal colours were shown with tight little wrap-around leather skirts.

Versace, still, despite the rising stars of Soprani and Ferre, second only to Armani in prestige, has, like Armani, been refining his line over the last few seasons, creating, season by season, clothes which are ever more feminine. Both his collection under his own name and the one he has a large part in, Callaghan, were predominantly narrow in line, with built-out shoulder pads to give a skinny, angular effect.

For autumn/winter 1983 the Milanese designers remained true

weekend fabrics to create clothes which were completely street-wise. Her long straight black corduroy skirts were teemed with grey herringbone tweed long semi-fitted jackets, a complete contrast to the almost New Look suits which followed them down the runway. Krizia's animal mascot for autumn is the bear, sometimes grizzly sometimes polar, but she paid a compliment to all the big cats when she dyed rabbit and knitwear to match the pelts of tigers, leopards, ocelots and cousins Nature never thought of.

Mandelli's cocktail wear is a successful combination of satin-striped, brightly coloured silk tunic coats over black velour dresses, while, for late evening, she develops her fine-pleated silver foil and adds vamp-like sequinned sheaths which are, if you catch my meaning, Holly-wood with good taste.

At Soprani sophistication lives after sunset. He showed some stunning slender dinner dresses with long sleeves and discreetly slashed backs secured at the neck with one fragile-looking button. The colours were black or white, the fabrics heavy crêpe or the heavy slipper satin which appeared in several collections.

The sexiest eveningwear, how-ever, is Gianni Versace's feather-to their instincts – and it showed in the confidence with which they presented their clothes. Sonia Rykiel, the French designer, may comment dismissively that the Italians lack that 'divine madness' which makes for true creativity in design as well as art. It's a debatable point but even if she is right, there's a lot to be said for Italian sanity and re-straint.●

NEW YORK

GLAMOUR REVISITED

● *By Bernadine Morris*

The world wide economic recession which catapulted the Italian designers into a frenzy of fancy design and propelled the British back to their roots has affected the Americans in another way. It has sent them on a straight and narrow path, avoiding the excesses of other seasons, and concentrating on the essentials. Good coats, suits and, to a lesser extent, dresses, abound for daytime wear. Glitter is paramount for evening, with truckloads of sequins decorating skinny skirts, sweaters and short shift dresses. But the shapes remain simple. Even for grand evenings, when just a season ago many designers presented bouffant skirts of an eighteenth century grandeur that Marie Antoinette or Scarlett O'Hara might have found appealing, simplicity prevails. The dominant long dress is a narrow one that clings to the body, has enough room for walking and, more often than not, covered shoulders. It may be paved in beads or sequins, but then designers must have some outlet for their extravagant ways.

What this amounts to is a renewed emphasis on what Americans call sportswear, though it has little to do with the playing fields. It is a workable concept of dressing, which can be applied to clothes for working women, an increasingly important category of fashion in a country where more than half the women over the age of 16 are employed outside the home and the number is increasing each year. It implies clothes that are easy to wear, non-restrictive and usually fairly casual. Many are made in separate parts which are interchangeable, thereby extending the ways in which the clothes are interchangeable, thereby extending the ways in which the clothes can be worn. Significantly, most of the best known designer names in American fashion are associated with sportswear.

Grey is the color of the season, as it is in other fashion centers, but it is varied in most collections by splashes of bold, bright colors, including rich blues, clear reds and a variety of stinging greens, along with cerise, yellow and almost every imaginable strong tone.

After a flirtation the previous season with skinny, hip-cupping skirts, inspired by or derived from the Paris designer, Azzedine Alaia, most designers have returned to easier shapes and longer lengths. Mid-calf to ankle length clothes dominate for day, though of course shorter, knee-baring styles are still available. Short skirts look kicky for evening, when they are usually shown with fancy stockings and high heel shoes. The woman who has dressed soberly during the day will enjoy kicking up her heels at night, the reasoning goes.

Somewhat surprising is the emphasis at most fashion houses on pants, which have certainly undergone a revival under the aegis of the best known designer names. Gone are the tricky bloused cuts, along with culottes and knee pants and other variants. What is important is the straight cut tailored trouser, sometimes tapering a bit and sometimes with pleats at the waist. It ties in with the sobriety that marks the season.

Perry Ellis shows the longest skirts throughout his collection, which is also the most innovative of the fall and winter season. The keynote is a highwaisted skirt or trousers. Barely grazing the waistband is the shortest of jackets, carried out in all kinds of fabrics from hand knits to furs. The result is a silhouette that looks faintly old-fashioned, though not identified with any particular period, and eminently young and perky. To give the look its particular swing, skirts and dresses are often made with multiple gores to flare out at the hem. Coats are also designed in this fitted and

PERRY ELLIS

flared shape, and cut long enough to barely clear the shoe tops.

This designer, who has never bothered with dressy clothes before, has added his first evening styles which were generally commended. The short, flyaway jacket now appears in bengaline over high-rising trousers. Short blouses in ivory crêpe top high-rising trousers. Short blouses in ivory crêpe top high-rising black velvet skirts. Sweaters have fur cuffs outlining bare shoulders. The evening clothes were widely commended. Mr. Ellis managed to add dressy elements without giving up his sportswear character.

Calvin Klein, who followed French sources rather too closely last season, showed an easier fit this time and returned to some of the clothes for which he is best known. The designer, who entered the fashion field as a coat designer in the 1960s before switching his attention to sportswear, showed excellent big tailored coats, colorful pea jackets and well designed knitted clothes, including sweater-jackets and dresses. His blazers were impressive in high colored satins as well as striped crêpe and black cashmere sweaters and looked elegant with long black taffeta skirts. As with Mr. Ellis, the sportswear theme was pronounced.

The Anne Klein collection, another of the leading sportswear lines, was also well-received. Designed by Donny Karan and Louis Dell'Olio since the founder's death a decade ago, the clothes have a hard-edged, snappy look. The designers have frequently combined black with brown for a sophisticated look, different enough from what other houses are presenting this season. Typical: brown leather skirt with black sweater or black fleece coat over a brown wool blouse. Fluffy angora sweaters, oversize

DONNY KARAN AND LOUIS DELL'OLIO FOR ANNE KLEIN

RALPH LAUREN

Argyle patterns in graphic black and white pullovers and short spangled skirts with velvet jackets for evening are some of the dramatic highlights of these slick clothes, enlivened by stinging shots of cerise in bolero jackets, with or without sequin accents.

Ralph Lauren, another of the sportswear leaders, faltered somewhat with his last collection. His British accent was as strong as ever in tweed jackets, shown with long pleated skirts or trousers. In a more playful view, he showed handknitted ski sweaters depicting skiers schussing down the slopes and ponchos in such sassy colors as chartreuse and cerise over black hooded tops and pants. His satin slip-top evening dresses with rhinestone straps suggested Jean Harlow and the golden days of the silver screen, but his knitted cashmere dresses with jewelled belts looked more contemporary.

There were indeed many good sportswear collections, including Adris with its air of ease in gracefully full bloused jackets and mohair sweaters, Gloria Sachs, with her revival of wool jersey in rich colors of wine and navy, and her sweaters which pick up colors and patterns of her silk jacquard or wool skirts and Blassport, the sportswear arm of the Bill Blass fashion empire. Blassport features sharply tailored casual clothes, such as jackets and coats in red and black plaids and white satin dinner jackets with grey flannel pants. They are clean, relaxed looks, mannish in inspiration, but somewhat softened for women.

To many observers, Geoffrey Beene embodies the best of American design. He is primarily concerned with the way clothes move with the body and how they feel. Even his most luxurious materials must be light in weight. Though he works at the most expensive end of the fashion spectrum, he is concerned with such practical matters as the fact that his clothes can pack without crushing or serve multiple functions through reversible fabrics.

There is a free-form feeling to his clothes this season. They are more supple than any other designers, taking their shape from the body of the wearer. Most of the clothes hang from big, rounded shoulders, and stop about the knees. Many dresses are reversible as well as jackets and coats.

There are no bright colors in the Beene collection, with the exception of red. He concentrates on the colors of anthracite, terra cotta and the earth. Basically, the clothes are simple and weightless. They reflect a contemporary attitude towards dressing.

Oscar De La Renta represents the other side of the coin. European in flavor, his clothes can be elaborately decorated: even his furs often have heavily embroidered borders. Day clothes are relatively subdued, though jackets can be encrusted with braid and velvet. Some of the simplest styles for evening are bright satin coats faced with black velvet and worn over short black velvet dresses. Beaded overblouses, sweaters paved with sequins and black dresses decorated with satin sashes draped diagonally across the chest are some of the less complicated styles for evening. The more sumptuous styles are loaded with embroidered beads and braid and appliques of lace. There is a market for these styles too among women who like to dress up.

The extensive panoply of American designers also includes many who are not easily categorized. Zoran's specialty is simple clothes in luxury fabrics such as cashmere which are made in one size to fit most bodies. He does not create a

CALVIN KLEIN

new collection each season, but merely adds to existing styles. A ribbed knitted cashmere top with a wide scooped neck and cap sleeves is his major contribution this time. His clothes are meant to be layered and interchanged. His color spectrum is narrow: black, white and grey.

Harriet Winter, who calls her business Mrs. H. Winter, began collecting and refurbishing antique clothes during the old clothes fervor of the 1960s. When that demand faded, she began designing her own clothes. She has developed a quirky individual style, producing clothes that cannot be mistaken for anyone else's. Her specialties are big coats with visible seams worn over jersey dresses. The coats have big shoulders achieved without pads. Her clothes have character, whether they are made of what looks like a

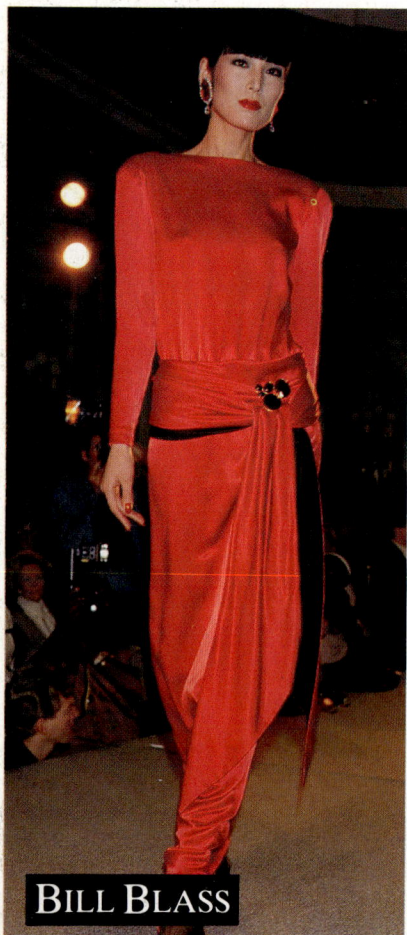

BILL BLASS

khaki army blanket or grey plastic-lined with black wool. She has just turned out one of her most inventive collections.

A show that failed because it didn't judge the temper of the times correctly was that of Willi Smith, a designer of young, unassuming clothes, in what was supposed to be a multi-media experience but was more like a happening of the 1969 variety, the designer invoked bizarre make-up, multiple television screens and an artsy craftsy atmosphere to present his clothes. They didn't stand up.

The mood of the American public is sober and realistic today. While a certain amount of extravagance in the manner of Oscar De La Renta can be absorbed, the emphasis is on traditional forms of clothes. There is little fantasy and little sense of abandon in the best received collections. But as many art forms prosper when the rules are strict, they are eminently suitable to contemporary life. It is a classic approach to fashion and it works well. There remains plenty of diversity, with both long and short jackets widely available, a choice of trousers or skirts and hemlines that cover most of the legs as well as those that bare the knees. There are fewer show-stoppers because designers simply can't afford to make clothes for shock value and the feeling is strong that even women who can spend a lot of money for clothes do not want to look flamboyant. Even sable coats are made in traditional shapes. The consensus is that women want their clothes to last more than a season. For customers who want to look different, there is always the imports from the Japanese or even the French. American designers are concentrating on clothes that look as if they will work and work for a long time.●

HALSTON

NORMA KAMALI

LONDON

SHALL WE SWING?

● *By Brenda Polan*

There are three schools of thought on the subject of London as a fashion centre. The first holds that it is no such thing; the second that it is the only true centre of creativity off which the rest of the international fashion community feeds, vampire-like; and the third falls somewhere in between and is flavoured with a substantial dose of frustration and even anger. For, owing to a fatal combination of British parochialism, British arrogance and that persistent compulsion to classify, stratify and specialise which is uniquely British, it is a fragmented and desperately inefficient industry. As in the nineteenth century, aestheticism (or creativity) and commerce are antipathetic; the same chap cannot be good at both and if he is, he must be a bounder.

There are, of course, exceptions since even Britain cannot resist the pace of change of the twentieth century; but except for the spurious unity of the sixties, the British fashion industry has never learned how to exploit its own vast potential and how to sell it to the world. No wonder the rest of the world can plunder that potential with impunity.

In keeping with Britain's tradition for educational excellence, we have the best schools for young designers but their training is, again, in keeping with British educational tradition, abstract, intellectualised, aesthetics-oriented. Technique and commerce take back seats. Young designers who value technique and commercial skills must learn them elsewhere after they have graduated and the foreigners, who can teach them best, – the French, the Italians, the Americans – await the graduates with open arms and ingratiating smiles.

Attempts by enlightened teachers like Professor Joanne Brogden at the Royal College of Art to shift the emphasis of their courses towards a more commercial approach, whilst encouraging, are doomed to futility when the vast major part of the domestic industry, conservative and blinkered, has no room for young designers to serve out their essential apprenticeships.

So young design school graduates who do not wish to work abroad and have not got the stomach for work in the mass-market rag trade or in the design teams of individualism-squashing giants like Marks and Spencer, listen to the uncritical enthusiasm of their friends and, with £500 from mum, launch their own-label collection. Pathetically underfinanced, commercially ignorant and frequently technically amateurish, they are mostly doomed to fail amidst much lamenting, wringing of hands and loud reproaches to all and sundry who should have recognised and supported talent (banks, the solvent part of the industry, government, anyone). But money tends to be canny, and while the British still have a great and sentimental regard for amateurism, the financial institutions only underwrite it as a glamorous tax loss. And there's more publicity in having a horse race or a tennis tournament named after you than trying to be the saviour of the British fashion industry.

But the British preference for gentlemen rather than players has harmed the fashion industry in one way. Nowhere else in the world would it be thought clever for the totally untrained and inexperienced to set themselves up in a professional business; nowhere else in the world would fashion journalists take pleasure in the story of a nurse who alleges she couldn't find sexy enough clothes so set about making some and her friends loved them so the rest of the world will too – and the pictures show garments of a terrifying home-dressmaking

BETTY JACKSON

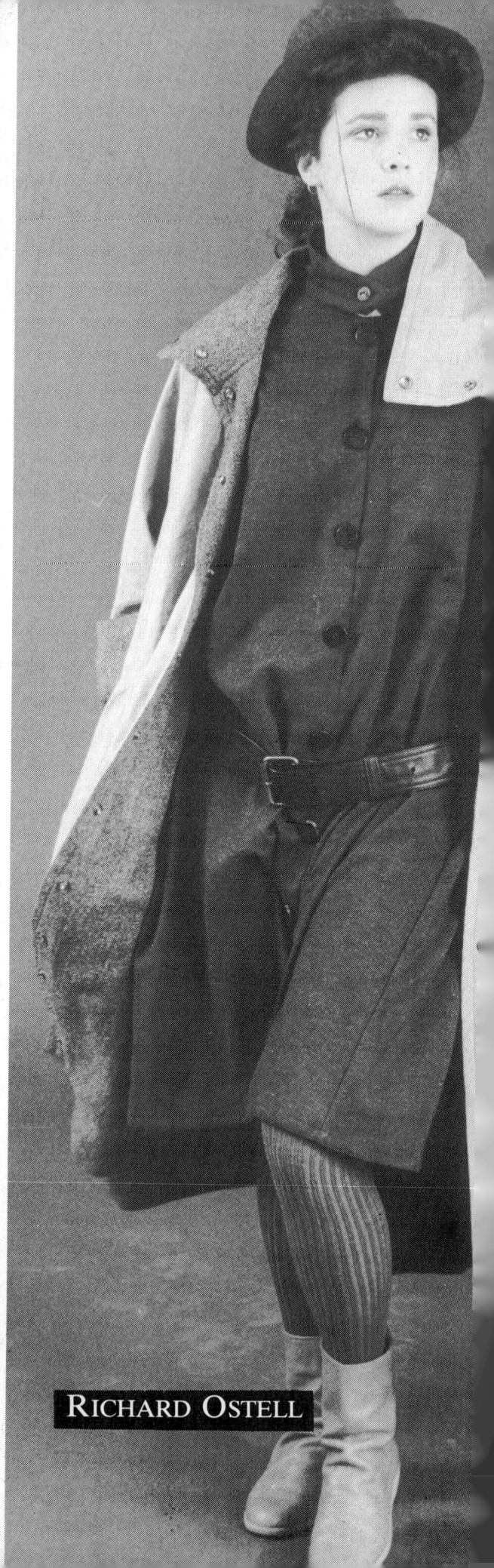

RICHARD OSTELL

JULIA PINES

amateurishness. When an industry and its commentators takes that kind of thing seriously, then it is not taking itself seriously and, as every psychiatrist and agony aunt knows, those who do not take themselves seriously will never be taken seriously by anyone else.

And the rest of the world takes the British fashion industry seriously only in one regard: its fertility. In December *Women's Wear Daily*, the New York-based and biased bible of the industry, took a major look at London. "This country," it summed up, "is a teeming fashion market-place buzzing with ideas." The article concentrated not on Britain's established designers, professional to their fingertips if often overcautious in the design statements they choose to make – Jean Muir, Janice Wainwright, Roland Klein, Hardy Amies, Bruce Oldfield, Zandra Rhodes – but on the eccentric young stylists taking their inspiration directly from the street, its tribes and every-changing but always iconoclastic modes of dress.

Down there at street level fashion is a living thing, an articulate extension of the psyche of the wearer, undiluted by the intervention of a designer or the cost limits of mass production or the taste limits of mass retailing. Down there Vivienne Westwood pouts sulkily and raises two fingers to the establishment and Steve Strange poses in yet another incarnation before his admirers, clustered and cloned in the 1930s cinema grandeur of the Camden Palace dance hall.

Young Britons have an understanding of the semiology of dress, an inborn sense of style and extraordinarily few inhibitions about expressing both. It is an insight and a talent uniquely British and it is rooted in the class system and its concomitant class struggle, the

THRIFT SHOP WAIF

RENAISSANCE SAVAGE

TATTERED, LAYERED WORKWEAR

MEAN STREETS FIFTIES

144

LEATHER BOY BUTCH

ART SCHOOL BAROQUE

THRIFT SHOP NEW LOOK

SHERIDAN BARNETT

violent clash of generation with generation which has become a pattern in the decades since World War Two, the need, in an urban society with a mobile population and few extended family or tribal ties, to create a peer group identity while remaining an individual within it. In other crowded, hostile cities, gangs of young people use dress as a secondary method of establishing loyalty and territory; force, physical brutality or the threat of it, is the primary method. In Britain the reverse tends to be true, so dress is uniquely important.

One result is the beginning of the shrugging off of the dead hand of Beau Brummel, the crony of the Prince Regent (later George IV) who ordained an end to display in dress for men. No longer would men use dress to define (except with esoteric subtlety of old school tie, Savile Row cut, pinkness of shirt) their status, express their sexuality, intimidate their inferiors or ingratiate themselves with their superiors. Instead, they would dress their wives and chattels and stand, Whistlerian studies in shades of grey and dun, proprietorially at their sides.

Among the young stylists of London street culture, the men have as much to say sartorially as the women do and the influence of both is evident in the work of Britain's street-wise designers and the international designers who are sensitive to this fertile source of stylistic ideas. And because the men dress as expressively as the women, there is an androgynous quality to British style.

Women have dressed as men for a long time. The Englishwoman in her hairy tweeds and Burberry mackintosh, a slightly feminised version of her lord and master down to her wellingtons, was a stock joke in Europe until Coco Chanel

redrew the clothes slightly and made them fashionably acceptable. The stamina, in fashion terms, of denim has a lot to do with the fact that what was originally male workwear was appropriated by, and looked sexy on, women. Even Shakespeare realised that the concept of woman dressed as man (even though the woman dressed as man was really a boy) was titillating and thought-provoking since it allowed the dramatist to challenge stereotypes. Literature has exploited the theme outrageously ever since.

What is new about the new androgynous factor in British fashion is that the men are appropriating elements of female dress even to the point of lavishly applied cosmetics. Ever since Mick Jagger sashayed on stage on a frock, youth culture has been doing exactly what he intended it to do, questioning its preconceptions about male dress and, by extension, female dress. Today not only frocks and mascara are quite common on male torsos and faces, but so are earrings, necklaces, pretty shoes, dyed and teased locks. Once, sighted in London's Soho, the wearers could have been quickly classified as homosexual or aberrant. Transvestism was a problem about which the sufferers wrote agonised letters to specialist magazines. Today's wearers are writing agonised letters to no one.

If the young Brits have turned assumptions about male and female dress on their heads, they have also inverted the status factor. It is unarguable that over the centuries dress has been used, as James Laver first explained, for two primary functions: to express status and power and to express sexuality and sexual availability or otherwise. The young Brits and the young Japanese who acknowledge a debt to them, have, in both cases, overturned the rules.

The pace-setters on the streets pushed one part of British fashion towards a development of the Hard Times workwear look: ill-fitting basic garments in rough, workaday fabrics, maltreated to look old, scruffy, impoverished. In tune with the Japanese, this is anti-status fashion and its direction is towards sobriety of colour, saggy, almost shapeless volume and great textural interest. Just as Zandra Rhodes took original Punk with its rips and safety pins and made it into disturbingly sexy eveningwear, so

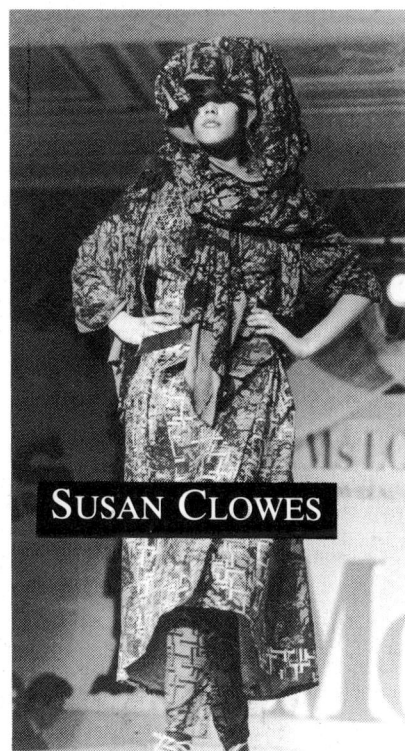

SUSAN CLOWES

designers like Katherine Hamnett and Darlajane Gilroy, Betty Jackson and Susan Clowes, Stephen Linard and Richard Ostell have taken the shapes, or the textures or just the mood of Hard Times and transformed them into clothes which, often sexy and always attractive, can be accepted by the majority who, while not feeling the need of the street stylists to distance themselves from and even alienate the rest of society, sense the mood of the times.

LA PALETTE

ALLY CAPELLINO

ROY PEACH

FRED SPURR

This anti-status, eclectically magpie style of dress was never clearer than in May when London Saluted New York with a show held quite suitably somewhere down off the Bowery with its tramps and drunks dressed in similarly anti-status style. Here, too, the androgynous qualities of the style were underlined as American and European fashion writers (those that made the effort to attend) anxiously demanded if their neighbour could guess the sex of the person on the runway.

The top end of the British fashion industry, which does not claim to lead, was divided for autumn between the classicists and the romantics. The influence from Paris, recoiling as it was from the impact of the Japanese, indicated a classical chic and designers like Jean Muir, Jasper Conran and Janice Wainwright had caught that mood. Others, like Roland Klein, whose autumn collection was probably his most impressive ever, were in a mood of lyrical romanticism – the great recurring theme in British design. This romanticism usually revolves around nostalgia for some Arcadian rural past; on this occasion, however, the nostalgia was for the sensuous, long-skirted linearity of the period when the first world war put paid to the suffragette movement while raising the consciousness of all the women dragged out of service and into munitions factories.

The shapes reflected that busy cross-pollination going on between Britain and Japan: large, often T-shaped jackets with deep armholes, simple shift dresses, a sense of texture dictating shape. Sheridan Barnett, who had always had an instinct for menswear fabrics, produced a collection he described as "classic, English, mixing marvellous tweeds in natural cream/

WINGROVE AND LEACH

ROLAND KLEIN

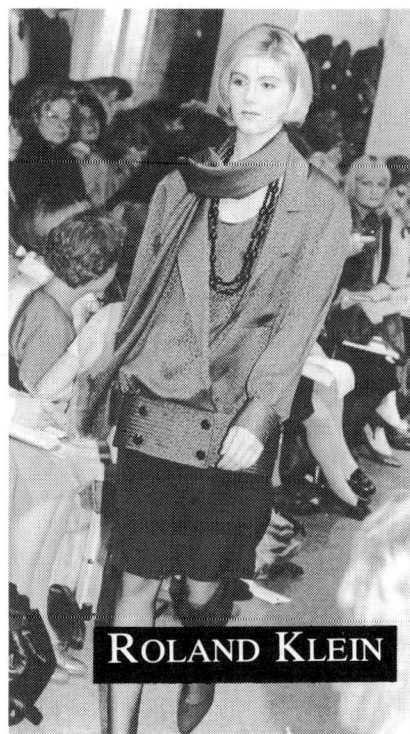

BRUCE OLDFIELD

grey/brown/charcoal Jacobs Wool, with handknits in the same wool and menswear shirtings to go with them, and grey flannel and big, very romantic coats, rather 1920s Russian in mood with wonderful oversized fur collars.''

Evenings, according to London's top eveningwear designers like Bruce Oldfield, Zandra Rhodes and David Sassoon and Belinda Belville of Belville Sassoon, were ultra-sophisticated with lots of sheaths or long-sleeved dinner dresses in slipper satin (predominantly oyster or black) and more than a touch of Hollywood glitz here and there.

In its range and its fertility, London offers fashion riches un-paralleled elsewhere in the world. But it brings to mind the poet's ''fine frenzy'' of creativity rather than the businessman's disciplined pro-ductivity. But then, despite all those calumnious myths spread abroad by the nation's enemies about a nation of shopkeepers, Britain has really always been better at the former. And it seems disinclined to study new ways.●

ZANDRA RHODES

GIORGIO ARMANI

THE LONER

● *By Brenda Polan*

L ike its music, its art, its favourite beverage, the names of its great fashion designers can summon to the nostalgic mind an entire period of time. If Chanel means the twenties, Dior the fifties and Quant the sixties, then Armani could come to mean the eighties. His clothes, like the clothes of Chanel and Dior, are way beyond the financial means of the larger part of the population – even his sportswear Emporio range is not cheap – but his importance lies in his influence on the rest of the industry.

Giorgio Armani, born in Piacenza, the son of Maria and Ugo Armani, a transport company manager, grew up during the second world war, its air raids and its privations. An early interest in the theatre was the result of trips backstage with his grandfather, a wigmaker, but parental pressure sent him to medical school. After three years he was called up and spent another three years as a medical assistant in the army. His patriotic duty done, Armani took a job, in 1954, at Rinascente, the large department store chain, working on window displays. Transferred to the office of Fashion and Style, he began to learn about fabrics and, more importantly, about the people who would spend money to wear them.

"It is one thing," he says, "to design clothes, but it is something else to hang around the salesrooms watching the public react to them. That rapport with the customer is very important to a designer." He can still be discovered serving in the Armani boutique in Via Sant' Andrea or in the Emporio shop opposite his offices in a seventeenth-century palazzo in Via Durini in Milan.

After seven years in Fashion and Style he left Rinascente to design menswear for Nino Cerruti who was later to tell Time magazine (which in

April, 1982 gave Armani its cover) that he could claim no credit for discovering Armani. "That's impossible because he discovered himself. He had a natural talent and he is self-taught. He would have stood out from the crowd in any case. Men like Armani are so rare that when one emerges even the blind are aware of it."

Cerruti, whose family firm manufactures fabric as well as clothes made from it, sent his new employee to spend a month in one of the factories. "There," says Armani, "I fell in love with textiles and began to understand the work behind each yard of fabric. That's why today, whenever I see anyone throwing away a sample of cloth, it's like cutting off my hand."

In 1970, a 25-year-old draughtsman with a Milanese architectural firm, Sergio Galeotti, persuaded Armani that he could go it alone as a designer. First he hired out his skills as a consultant to other manufacturers, then, in 1975, he finally launched his own label in a tiny office with a few chairs and one huge table.

Eight years later he looks, despite his faded jeans, plain white Emporio T-shirt and scuffed leather jacket, as if he has never worked anywhere else but beneath the high frescoed ceilings of the Palazzo Durini. He has three homes: a Milan apartment a short walk from Durini, its décor austere, a converted farmhouse, which he owns with Galeotti, in Forte dei Marmi, three hours from Milan, and a Moorish-style house on the island of Pantelleria, 50 miles off the Tunisian coast.

He is a serious man, and a hard-working one. Besides his much-coveted ranges of Giorgio Armani clothes for women and for men, he designs the slightly cheaper Mani collection, the Erreuno collection and the Mario Valentino collection (not to be confused with Valentino of Rome who has recently opened his own shop in Sloane Street, Knightsbridge) which are all womenswear ranges and the Armani Emporio sportswear ranges for men and women. There are 52 Emporio shops in Italy and, although the Americans are anxious to get their hands on this less expensive range, he will not let them have it until he can manufacture in the US and keep prices down. For the first time Browns in South Molton Street, London, are stocking Emporio this spring.

In the reorganisation of the string of South Molton Street shops, Browns has, in fact, given Armani star billing with a shop to himself — Emporio downstairs and Armani and Mani on the ground floor. To a certain extent (muscle-bound dollars must be taken into consideration) it reflects the durability of the Italian master compared to the more fleeting charms of the New Worlder whose space Armani has moved over to fill: Calvin Klein.

At his best, Klein can make clothes with the same sense of modernity which pervades Armani's work, but never with the same perfectionism, consistency of approach and sheer, simple intelligence. Armani is not coy. "My clothes," he says, unregretfully, "are for women who have money. They are not for a teenager who expects novelty; she could not afford them and the quality would be wasted on her since she does not want to keep anything long. Too much of fashion is aimed at her, so that mature women start to think that, since that is nearly all there is, they must wear it too.

"I hate most of all the idea of women trying to look like children, trying to be a baby doll. So women like to look younger, that is natural, but the general trend is for women to try and look like children and that is unnatural. Adults should know how to accept ageing and a fashion

industry should not force adults to masquerade as children. There has been an over-emphasis in recent fashion on youth and amusement.

"Sometimes you see a woman on the street and from the back she looks like a teenager. Then she turns and her face is that of a middle-aged woman, and it is a terrible shock," he says, serious-faced and not looking at all shocked. His own designs for spring and summer are certainly grown-up without being in any way staid or middle-aged and the ones for next autumn and winter are drawn along the sparest lines since the space-age futurism seen in Paris in the mid-sixties.

To eyes used to bulk, rich details, layers and clutter, the new collection is like a horizonless view of the ocean after a rather gaudy carnival scene.

This move towards refinement of line and mass has been developing in Armani's work through several seasons and it is one reason why an Armani is instantly distinguishable from the work of any other designer. He says: "Fashion has been over-charging its ideas in recent years. It

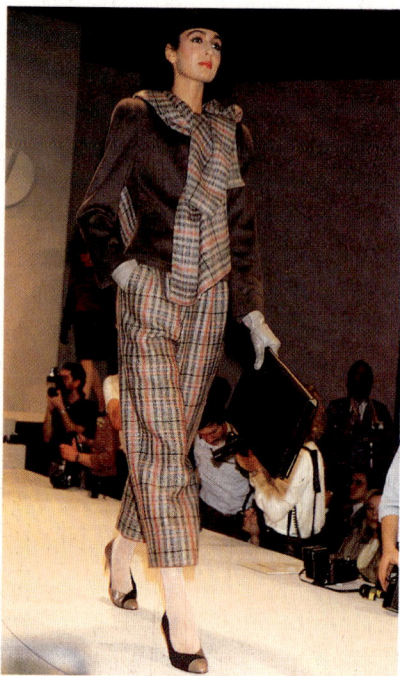

■ *Above: Erreuno, autumn/winter. Below: Giorgio Armani, autumn/winter. Opposite: Giorgio Armani, autumn/winter*

has become too much showbiz. Somehow clothes have become too intrusive and the wearer's personality disappears behind them. It is time to return to the basic principles of stylish dressing. I was aiming for simplicity and purity while very carefully avoiding banality.''

When press and buyers first glimpsed the severity of the new Armani line displayed, as the Armani collection has been displayed for the last three season, as a still life against dark horizontal panelling, they were, in Armani's words, a little shocked. Time and a closer inspection lifted their spirits. ''There are many collections in one collection,'' says Armani, ''and very many women, whatever the age, shape or size, but of a certain mind and sensitivity, will respond to the modernity of the collection, its adaptability to personal style. The clothes can look formal, but then a woman changes her high-heeled shoes for flatter ones, takes off her

hat, puts on a different belt and the clothes become realistic, more everyday.

''That is why I cannot do a runway show because that kind of presentation must make a statement, a big statement because it is a big runway and there are thousands in the hall. With the display and with the video which shows women walking along the street, in the home, in the car, I can show the clothes many ways and as part of real life.''

Seen that way, the clothes which look so abstract, so stylised against the dark slats, are alive, confident, easy. They are consistent with his ambitions when he launched that first collection in 1975. Fashion then was a schizophrenic: ethnic hippiedom, all beads, rich peasants, Indian

scarves and earth mothers; and restricting outworn couture clichés translated into 'classics'. Something fresh was needed, Armani decided – something, as he puts it, ''a little used, not absolutely perfect''.

He was aiming for a relaxed style of dress which somehow had the insouciance of much-washed denim jeans and the elegance of a style of dress which no longer fitted into the lives of modern men and women. To this end he gave women the big blouson, almost mannish in cut, which automatically makes a woman square her shoulders, dig her hands into her pockets and adopt an aggressive stance. He layered fabrics, contrasting colour, pattern, texture, giving clothes at the same time an aura of medieval richness

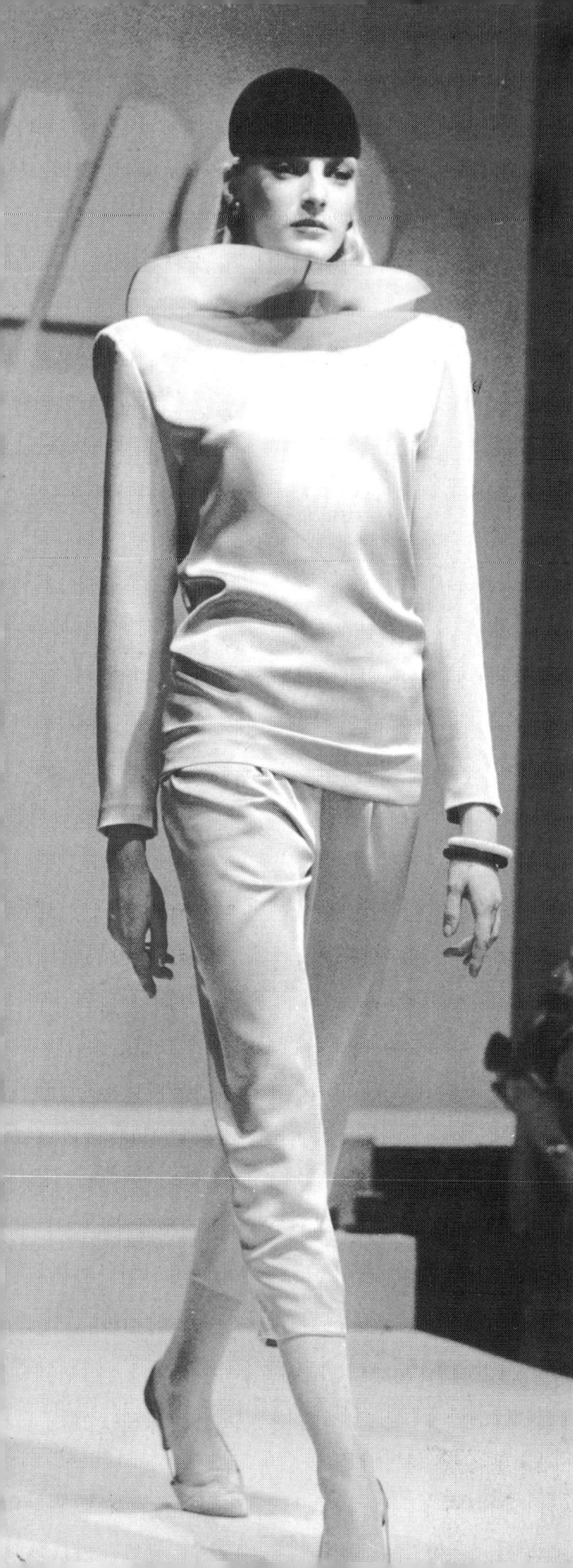

■ *Sci-fi satin evening suit, printed velvet shift and Prince of Wales tweed by Armani for Erreuno, autumn/winter*

and presence and a sense of light-hearted playfulness.

Together with other Italian designers like Versace, he brought leather, soft, supple, glistening, into the everyday wardrobe, teaming leather pants with a gabardine jacket, stitching suede into an eye-deceiving plaid, popping a leather gilet over a tailored coat. But the wit, the Milanese cool with which he did it was all his own.

He redefined fit, allowing blouses and blouson jackets to droop softly at the front in controlled but accidental-looking curves of fabric which emphasised the beauty of the fabric and took all the formality out of tailoring.

Armani has little truck with the grand life, the fuss and pretention which afflict some of his peers; some even call him moody, reclusive. He is merely serious and lacking in content. He told *Time:* "My ideas may come from unimportant things, from a book, a film, from talking to my staff or from watching how people behave and live. I cannot allow myself the luxury of waiting for the moment of inspiration. I design clothes that can be designed at a certain cost, that can be sold and can be worn.

"The beginning of a new collection is a drama. But eventually, without being theatrical, without drinking or smoking or listening to background music. I just begin to design on a sheet of white paper." What appears on that sheet of paper, the wonderful colourings, the sureness with pattern and texture, the superb unstructured structure, the easy-ness of Armani, is the wise-money bet for theme for the 1980s.●

■ *Azzedine Alaia with model and (inset) with constant companion*

AZZEDINE ALAIA

THE EXOTIC

● *By Marina Sturdza*

The rue de Bellechasse is a quiet unhurried thoroughfare, a small oasis of calm in the heart of St. Germain des Prés. But at number 60, behind the unassuming nameplate that reads simply 'Alaia', life is chaotic, total bedlam. Telephones shrill incessantly. Top-ranked arbiters of international fashion are lined up on every level of the dark, tortuous staircase, like so many audition hopefuls, patiently awaiting entrée into what must be the world's tiniest showroom. Eventually, they'll be sandwiched into a cramped antechamber and finally allowed to observe the latest creations of Azzedine Alaia, easily the most successful designer in Paris today, and arguably the most influential force in fashion of the past few seasons.

Pandemonium has reigned ever since Alaia's 'discovery' by the international press and fashion elite, some three seasons ago. In fact, long before his latest discovery and the rivers of delirious prose he's inspired, long before he was lionized by the press and long before the world at large began lining up on his doorstep, Alaia was already a success by any calculation. His address has been a loosely kept secret of the Paris cognoscenti (such as internationally acclaimed interior designer Andrée Putman, or the super-avant-garde editors of *Elle* magazine) for at least a decade.

That's why it's a giggle to see the beau monde of fashion, press and buyers alike, rank and position regardless, protocol be damned, crammed by the dozen into a meagre space intended to accommodate a very few at best; craning and jostling to catch even a glimpse of Alaia's models as they sporadically flash by. In fact, it's not a showroom at all, it's Alaia's apartment, long since transformed into workroom/office/dressing room/ and feeding station. The bed lies under the drawing board, the drawing board is buried under an ocean of paper, the models dress in an antechamber, the international buyers are stacked in the vestibule, and life during the prêt-à-porter collections has become a round-the-clock state of siege. Privacy, or any semblance of a normal life for Alaia and his team (who have moved in for the duration) long ago fell by the wayside. No one can remember when they last slept and whenever things become totally impossible, the staff takes refuge in the kitchen or bathroom.

Not long ago, Alaia went out to buy french fries for his ravenous models and managed to lock himself out. In the confusion, no one even noticed his disappearance, and no one paid heed to his insistent pounding on the door, or his shouts from the street. Eventually, he was obliged to phone from the café next door.

The decibel level is pitched at an ear-splitting high. Buyers look distraught. Influential editors meekly await their turn to see Alaia. There's no point in complaining. Alaia is the hottest ticket in town and he knows it. The man of the moment is a pint-sized, compact personage, wearing a slightly bemused air under a mop of tightly curled hair, perpetually clutching a small, yappy dog. The dazed air is deceptive. Behind it is a man who's entirely aware of the power he currently wields and who thinks the whole trip is a delicious joke. Although he revels in it, he's not about to take the adulation too seriously; he's seen press and buyers come and go. It's a big mistake to underestimate Alaia. Behind the street urchin's grin is a steel-trap mind, one that registers every foible and pretension with wicked accuracy, the better to regale his cohorts later.

Why all the fuss, all the attention and all the sycophantic hangers-on, and why is Alaia so firmly ensconced as fashion's newest darling? Effectively, he has reinvented the shape of clothes. His designs are a celebration of the female shape, they delight in every female curve and line, without exaggeration, without costumery or caricature. In fact, his design premise is simplicity itself. Alaia marries fabric to the female body, with respect and with pleasure. His clothes are instantly recognizable, utterly different from anyone else's.

He moulds and manipulates even strong-textured fabrics on to the female shape, like a second skin. Silhouette and shape are everything, and the body itself is his essential inspiration. Alaia's clothes are light-years away from anything that smacks of trendiness and he doesn't give a fig about fads or 'what's in'. His clothes are frankly and unabashedly sexy and women adore them. They feel wonderful, and look even better, and they're

walking right out of the stores around the world.

Alaia, a man of indeterminate age, ("I am as old as the pharoahs") will, when pressed, admit that he was born in Tunis and came to Paris at 18 to study sculpture at the

■ *This page and opposite: three outfits by Alaia autumn/winter*

Beaux-Arts. A friend who'd recognized his native talent introduced him to the House of Dior, an establishment in which he lasted exactly five days, something of a short-lived record. Money was scarce, if not non-existent. Alaia paid for the maid's room he lived in by making clothes for the concierge. He had nothing, no stock, no samples, no help and no fabric, and little training – nothing but a small sewing machine he'd bought on credit. Apparently, that didn't stop some adventurous Parisian women (ever in search of *the* perfect garment) from wending their way to his attic room.

Eventually, Alaia moved to accommodate his expanding clientele. Word of mouth spread his reputation and soon drew him to the attention of *Elle* editor, Nicole

Crassat, immensely influential in the French fashion world, as well as Claude Brouet, the highly respected editor of *Marie-Claire*. Soon, everyone who was anyone in the French fashion business owned at least one Alaia, and his accessories sold like the proverbial hotcakes. It didn't take long for the international press and fashion industry to note that the French fashionables all seemed to sport what appeared to be a uniform designed by Alaia – body-defining, intensely revealing clothes in the softest, supplest leathers and sensuous knits, mostly trimmed with reams of studs and grommets (an Alaia detail that ran rampant several seasons ago). A major feature by Crassat in *Elle*, and a photospread in *Women's Wear*, by New York's talented Bill Cunningham, whose eagle eye had long ago discerned Alaia's abilities, finally tipped the balance and pushed him squarely into the limelight.

Behind the smokescreen of his frenetic activity and the apparent pandemonium Alaia is, in fact, splendidly organized. He has managed to meet the immensely increased demand and successfully complete all his deliveries. Most of his clothes are manufactured in France, leatherwear by Mac-Douglass, knitwear in Italy. While Alaia is delighted to see his clothes turn up on the backs of influential women, and spread across television screens and magazine layouts from Hong Kong to Los Angeles, he's not overly impressed with his own importance. His clothes are now available in about fifty prestigious stores throughout the world – in England at Brown's and at Joseph.

"I don't really care; I never have. It hasn't changed my life that much – I've always been busy; now I'm just more busy. I've never had any possessions, and in this mess I can't find anything anyway. I've never had time for a holiday and I can sleep anywhere. If everything changes tomorrow, I won't give a damn."

What he does care about is the five people he works with most closely. In fact, he won't go anywhere without his entourage, and when he does agree to travel, he demands the best. "If I go anywhere, it has to be perfect – I insist on being taken care of like a mistress . . . not like a wife," Alaia coyly stipulates with a wicked little grin. The last time he was persuaded to travel was at Bergdorf Goodman's behest in November, 1982 – his first trip to New York. He loved it, but complains that in ten days he saw only the store, his hotel and a few restaurants. Says Alaia: "I could live anywhere. I left the camels and slippers of Tunis for Paris. Right now, I'm French. Paris is still the centre, but I could just as well go to New York or Japan."

In fact, Alaia loves all things Japanese, the food, the decor and especially the deferential fashion editors. Alaia has strong opinions about everything, fashion in particular. On fashion: "Fashion is impossible to define. So is beauty. A woman can be beautiful on the exterior but ugly inside. Beauty can be large or small – who cares? For me, beauty is personality, being alive. I stress the body and I have to try my things on a living body because the clothes I make must respect the body. I don't care if it's long or short; I don't pay attention to trends, but, whatever you do, big shoulders or small, they must sit right on the shoulder and respect its natural movement.

"I don't pay attention to what others are doing and I'm not

interested in what I did last year, last season, or even yesterday. What I did yesterday, I've already forgotten."

He's also got firm ideas about fashion merchandising. His fall, 1983 collection, including some 50 models, all in rich alpaca, cashmere, wool, silk and skin-thin, luxurious suede and leather is an international sellout, even though Alaia adamantly refuses all requests for exclusivity, special contracts or licensee arrangements. He's 100 per cent in control, 100 per cent free to do exactly as he pleases – a privilege

he exercises with great glee. "If it's good and women want it – they don't care about exclusivity."

Alaia's autumn 1983 colorations were all deep and intense – charcoal, burnt umber, indigo, black and dark forest green which he freely mixes and matches. If his clothes have previously stressed curves, this year they are even more clearly underlined with wrapped effects further delineating the derrière; clingy, sheer knits outlining the bosom and waist; supple featherweight leathers and suedes positively cupping every curve. These sleek looks slide under strong, chevronned ribbed or brushed wools and leathers – some in oversize plaids, some in colour-matched solids – bold-shouldered coats and jackets, some cropped at the waist, some hip-length, three-quarter-length, or seven-eighths-length, or to mid-calf.

Alaia rarely differentiates between day and evening looks, though he does give a nod to late-day with a couple of bare evening knits and a virtually transparent sheer cashmere djellaba in brilliant purple. The complementary accessories are stunning: curvaceous suede gloves that are wrapped and furled to mid-arm, featherweight cashmere hose and elegant suede or leather pumps, all coloured to match the clothing.

While Alaia's prices are fast approaching the stratosphere, in part because he uses only the finest natural fibres and pays top dollar to the prestigious manufacturers who produce his goods, even the less affluent can afford an Alaia. The inexpensive clothes and accessories he designs for Les Trois Suisses, a Sears, Roebuck-style catalogue giant, sell out almost instantly, making Alaia designs accessible even to the rabidly fashion-conscious masses.●

■ *This page and opposite: two outfits by Alaia autumn/winter*

COUTURE

THE ALCHEMIST'S LABORATORY

● *By Serena Sinclair*

The press often manages to give the impression that each six-monthly Prêt-à-Porter revelation comes as a complete surprise. What's up, what's down, what's in, what's out . . . As you read their copy you can envisage them, poised on the edge of their seats, breath bated, newshound instinct alert to be the first to bring word of the "new line" to their readers.

But they, and their readers, need not be taken by surprise. Now, in 1983, more than ever before, each ready-to-wear collection is presaged by the couture collection of the previous season. Because of the time involved in the manufacture of ready-to-wear and its delivery to shops and boutiques all over the world, those collections are shown a good half-year before they will be in the shops. The couture collection is shown three months later.

It is the couture collection which gives the designer room to experiment. It is into the couture collection that he puts his fresh ideas, his sometimes outrageous, often provocative thoughts on the way ahead for fashion. This was never clearer than this year when an inspection of January's spring-summer couture collections clearly pointed the way to this March's autumn-winter ready-to-wear collections.

The year dawned bright for the world of Paris couture. Fashion was in the process of swinging back to elegance and elegance is what the French couturiers know about. Even the whackiest back-street manufacturer was talking sleek, slim skirts, fitted jackets, the return of the sculpted dress. For the couture men and women, this was gravy time.

In January they scissored their way into one of the most handsome fashion seasons they had ever achieved. This was Paris as Paris ought to be. It was chic fashion; it was, in some instances, hard

fashion. Paris hasn't been a soft city since the days of Clovis and Ste Geneviève when earthy browns in rustic weave were the thing.

Abandoned, this year, were all the earth-mother cosy clothes. Ignored (perhaps at peril?) was the whole rising tide of Japanese workwear, tattered bag-lady fashion which was giving the ready-to-wear men of Paris a few sleepless nights (to follow? to ignore? to swamp?). Even the longer skirt, beloved of the young fashion-followers, got short shrift in Paris couture. Ungaro did a few mid-calf party dresses, Cardin some batwing-top silk prints reaching to four inches below the knee. But the knee-top day skirt won all around the houses, with Ungaro's firmly three inches above the knee, somewhat to the consternation of clients like Olympia Rothschild who averred that a few changes would have to be made when she placed *her* order.

The newest skirt in Paris in January was the tulip wrap, sometimes so half-heartedly wrapped that it swirled open like something on a musical comedy stage. Lanvin did some beauties. The tulip and waterfall wrap skirts, often asymmetric (as was much else in Paris) were further dramatised by hip-swagging and draping, especially at Ungaro. Lanvin's bustle on a taffeta dress was more hip excitement and the talk of Paris.

The couture was happily doing the things the mass-manufacturers just cannot do with their orders for a thousand dresses and machines to keep busy. All the work of loving hands, of skilled craftswomen in small ateliers, was much in evidence and sportive styles took a back seat to a more formal elegance. So powerful was the feeling for traditional French chic engendered by these collections, it pervaded the following ready-to-wear, bringing the tulip skirt and tailored jacket

■ Ungaro's traditional
Parisian chic: slim
silhouette, above-the-
knee hemline

into the boutiques for autumn, their acceptance assured by their success in January.

The wide rever was another strong symbol of the Paris couture season and most of all in white pique, winging out almost to shoulder bone. This is not really career-girl fashion – not strap-hanging career girl anyhow – and benefits from the daily attention of a ladies' maid. The white rever showed best on snug-fitting long suit jackets at Dior and the best were usually a contrast, such as big black and white plaid for the jacket, tiny checks for the skirt. Ungaro, one of the few sources of colour in a sombre season, favoured bright yellow jackets piped in black, to match the skirt, and further dazzled the eye with red blouse and turquoise belt.

What, no blouses? Paris abandoned them, on the whole,

■ *Above: Maryll Lanvin's asymmetric summer sheath dress. Right: Marc Bohan's wide-lapelled tailored suit for Dior. Far Right: Ungaro's Fortuny pleated swathed tubular evening dress*

though if you're going to have a blouse, Ungaro's are the ones to watch, as ever. The suit neck, very décolleté was instead filled in with giant beads of crystal and jet, cabuchon fake rubies and sapphires. The look recalled the late 1940s and early '50s when women wore those no-blouse suits in severe black gabardine or whipcord.

Spencer jackets, matador jackets, boleros all shifted the eye upwards and looked newer than any of the still-lingering blousons. Yet another upward signal came from Cardin with his Empire-belted dresses, his skirts with high matador waistlines. The French, with cool regard for fashion-in-the-headlines, called these highwaisted garments 'Argentines'. Ungaro's short jackets looked like bellhops' with their snappy vest points and could lead to a lot of confusion. But couture customers are used to this: both Ungaro and Saint Laurent did bellhop jackets the previous year.

A dress certain to be loved by

■ *Above: Yves Saint-Laurent's narrow seven-eighths coat over short straight skirt. Right: Yves Saint-Laurent's slipper satin evening sheath*

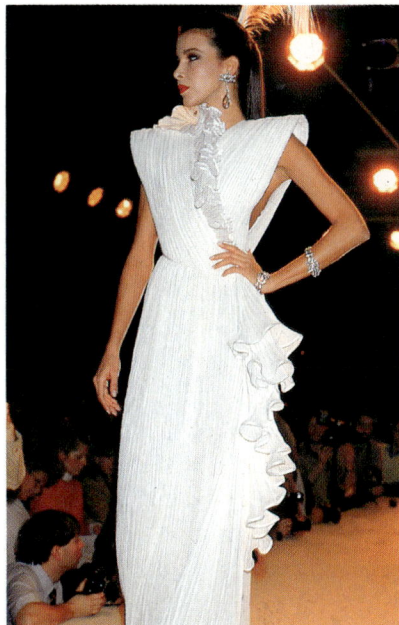

■ *Left: Hubert de Givenchy's tulip-skirted narrow dress. Above: Emanuel Ungaro's slender white column of an evening dress*

many women of uncertain waistline was the straight up-and-down coat dress and everyone showed it. Saint Laurent's were particular charmers, including the black velvet with a deep slanting V neckline and a tulip wrap sexy skirt. And, although the occasional suit was belted (Cardin remained faithful to his peplum line), many dresses were not. The low hipline sash was much seen and the simple shift with gathers springing from a loose hipline seam.

Black and white dominated the Paris spring scene and what brights there were turned out to be hard brights: red, hot yellow, cobalt. The rare look of old-fashioned prettiness came from that old maestro, Givenchy, now celebrating his 30th year in couture, who did a bouquet of square-necked floral print silk dresses with huge bell sleeves chopped above the elbow and full dirndl skirts. His ballgowns (a rare commodity now in Paris) were shaped in the same bouffant immensely flattering way.

171

Plain fabrics provided socko glamour in Paris evening clothes, like the pale grey slipper satin from Saint Laurent, a slim column with gently swathed bust, and the all-pleated Grecian-look white crepe from Ungaro, hugging the figure as ardently as a mummy's swathing. These are dresses that stay in the memory of fashion-watchers and which people can recall, with pleasure, even years later.

There was a new erogenous zone in Paris couture and guess what – for a change it was not the deep front plunge, the cinched waist, the draped hip. It was the under-arm area. Dresses were slashed down to waist level under the arms and there you were: choosing between a lacy bra, a beautiful satin camisole, a silk T-shirt under your dress, or total exposure to the waiter passing the claret.

Who's buying all this grandeur? Some 3000 women round the world, that's who, of which 50% are American, 20% Gulf Arabs, 10% French. The sales turnover for combined couture and couturiers' boutique clothes totals some 800 million francs a year. Vogue Patterns are the biggest commercial customers, far exceeding the manufacturers and the small boutiques who buy a muslin toile for copying. Once there were hundreds of these but when the couture men started doing their very own prêt-à-porter it killed that particular golden goose, but in the process spun out a lot more money for the original creators.

Paris couture collections, once the big January and July shows are over, don't just remain placidly in Paris. They're on the trot a great deal of the time, shepherded by the staff of one fashion house (i.e. Givenchy showing his spring collection to 30,000 cheering Japanese in Tokyo, Ricci taking theirs to show

in the Kremlin) or by the press officer of the Chambre Syndicale, the group all the couture houses belong to. She spends much of her life swaddled in tissue paper with microphones attendant, packing up the clothes after big tours of Latin America or Texas and being interviewed by local press and TV. 1983's dates included Rome in April, Tokyo, Osaka and Hongkong in November.

Good effects of these big couture shows in the outlying fashion spots of the world are not, of course, limited to actual couture purchases. Perfume sales shoot up, the scarves whistle out of the department stores, the designer's own ready-to-wear feels the impact.

And that's what much of couture boils down to, in the end: a great showcase, a publicity machine, "a diva, a superstar" as the French put it, a high standard of breathtaking excellence to ginger up the sales of all these hundreds of offshoots a couture house has, and lives by. The more and better publicity a collection has, the better chance a new perfume, about to be launched, has to succeed. (Oddly enough, exceptions prove the rule: almost no one writes about Paco Rabanne yet his

■ *Left: Pierre Cardin's high-waisted long sack dress. Above: Marc Bohan's trompe l'oeil wide leather false lapels on his big three-quarter length swagger coat for Dior*

Calandre is a beloved steady seller.)

The spin-offs are myriad. The designer, and they all admit it, needs the freedom of the hang-the-expense couture collection to experiment with new cuts, extraordinary fabrics (some costing £150 a metre like the embroidered organzas from St. Gall). This experimentation, once it proves that it works on figures great and small, is then adapted, watered-down if you like, for the prêt-à-porter collection which follows three months later. There you see the clothes as the big machines can handle them, not as they are made by loving, utterly absorbed hand-workers in the upstairs atelier.

Every craft, every profession, needs its lodestar, its pinnacle, and for the vast world of fashion, Paris couture is just that. But it is also the laboratory, the crucible in which the near future is shaped. Watch Paris couture and know whither the rest of the fashion world is about to head. ●

173

MODELS

THE FACES ABOVE THE CLOTHES

● *By Jackie Modlinger*

There was a time when the model-girl was as much of a star as the Hollywood heroine herself. In the late fifties and early sixties, the definitive clothes-horse was that well-bred young lady from the upper echelons of society, even if, like Tania Mallett, she sported plimsolls with a hole in the toe.

The Sixties spawned famous faces like Jean Shrimpton, Celia Hammond, Sandra Paul, Penny Patrick and Moyra Swan. The Seventies was Maudie James, Ingrid Boulting, Barbara Miller and the Pygmalion of the modelling world, Twiggy, a brilliant product of Justin de Villeneuve, her Svengali. All household names. But ask your average person the name of a top model these days, and they'll probably say Marie Helvin or Jerry Hall if you're lucky. Though both these girls have been around for some time, now, they tend to make headlines more for the company they keep, rather than the job they do.

The last model who made any impact was Kelly Le Brock. She went to New York and took it by storm. You used to be able to label a girl, put a face to a year, a style too. But no longer. Now it's a question of looks, and finding the label that fits the look. 1982 was the year of the spikey-haired clone or, alternatively, by way of a contrast, The all-American Prairie Girl. Hard put to attribute a name to the latter, if pushed, I have to give redhead Kathy Coulter my accolade for last year.

Defining The Face of '83 is something of a tall order. Because no single face mirrors this year, 1983 must of necessity, reflect the order, style and fashion of the day. Fashion is not single-minded rather multi-directional. Fashion today has many faces, therefore it is only logical that those girls who wear contemporary clothes must both complement and reflect its multi-faceted mood. Since there is no one definitive look or trend in fashion for '83, the faces that mirror it must reflect this mood. And so there is not just one face, but several.

In short, it is a question of clothes-horses for courses. The Face of '83 must be able to both reflect and project the look that she is wearing. And no one girl can encapsulate all the different looks.

Given this broad spectrum, The Face of '83 can be summed up in a single word – individual, like fashion itself. And since it is the model agents who call the tune, and dictate the looks, over to some of them for confirmation that individuality is indeed the name of the '83 game:

Says Chrissie Castagnetti of Select Agency: "It is very much an individual look; an individual face, not all teeth and smiley, and not this clone-look where all the girls looked alike. A year ago, it was all full mouths, then all teeth, an American look. Today, the model must have her own individuality that shines through," she says.

"There is that infant look – one of pure innocence, and diametrically opposed to it, another completely different look of untouched sensuality. . . . And there are no hard and fast rules – some girls suit the 'Bob' hairstyle; others look better with short hair, like Liz Adams. We don't follow a 'look', we go on what suits the girl, not what look happens to be 'in' because I don't believe there is an 'in' look," she confides.

Says the boss of Models One, Jo Fonseca: "Beautiful, feminine, individual . . . the individual look is coming back . . . that all-blonde, toothy grin is going out," she insists.

As part of the 'Britain Salutes New York' promotion earlier this year, Models One sent out several of their models to promote a new look in English beauty. Believes Jo: "In the 60's, it was international, in the 70's Ingrid Boulting; now

there's a new breed – like Joanne Russell, Maria Johnston, they're the new English Roses. They're so English and have such a fantastic fineness about their faces and bones. There's so much mixed blood in America, which we don't have here . . . the English race are so pure, and it's a much more refined look, not so toothy and a better skin. I think that the English look is coming in, that all-American, blonde, sporty style is on the wane," says Jo.

Says Mary-Ann Edgar, erstwhile talent-scout at Models One Agency: "The Face of '83 is much less the American look, blonde, sporty, wonderful smiles, fresh and beachy.

"Now it is far more individual and girls have more character in their faces so they can be more recognisable. The look is sexier, not in a sleazy way, but things like that generous mouth, almost a young Bardot, though you don't have to be blonde with lean legs; it is something more sensual, more subjective . . . it isn't a matter of being lean now, maybe they have a more womanly figure, they have after all, to relate to the woman in the street, that's who they're talking to . . . yes, a more natural figure and one that the woman in the street can identify with. . ." confirms Ms. Edgar.

All three underscore the feeling and subscribe to the individualist school.

Since in the Eighties, fashion inspiration stems from the street, it is here that the models of the

■ *From left: Rachel Riley, 18, reading social anthropology at New Hall, Cambridge; Louise Rettie, 19, reading law at Christ College, Cambridge, Kathy Coulter, 21, reading English at Jesus College, Oxford; Julliette Towhidi, 19, reading languages at New College, Oxford.*

moment are to be scouted. Far from being superstars, they are just down-to-earth girls, who possess, above all else, street-awareness. A new reality is creeping into this world of so-called glamour.

A schoolgirl, secretary or university undergraduate can be model-girl material. She can and frequently does step straight off the street or come from the Provinces into a London agency, and, if she has the potential, become a successful model virtually overnight. Which is just what is happening. And the case of the three faces I have chosen as The Faces of '83.

New, too, is the blossoming of the Bluestockinged Beauty. A handful of young models who are Oxbridge undergraduates and model during their holidays. This provides an excellent way of subsidising their degree courses, and the fact that availability is restricted in this way means that they do not run the risk of over-exposure.

Says make-up artist, Mark Hayles, who created the make-up for the pictures for two of our three '83 faces: "The Face of '83 can be one of two things – very sophisticated of natural and healthy . . . it is like fashion, it can go in any direction, at the moment . . . a woman has many faces, and the face of '83 is one that can look versatile, change with the mood . . . demure or very ethnic.

"The Face of '83 has to be a face to suit the mood because there are so many moods around," he believes.

Who, then epitomizes The Face of '83? Take 3 girls – they just happen, purely by chance, to be a Blonde, Kathryn Hardy, Irish brunette, Deborah Hanna, and red-head, Venita Marshall.

Just over a year ago, KATHRYN HARDY was just a 16-year-old schoolgirl studying for her 'O' levels along with other schoolgirls of her

generation. In just one year, this bobbed, blonde young lady with a pouty, 'Bardot-esque' expression has been catapulted to Cover-Girl par excellence and top international model. And I had to go to Paris where she was working to photograph her.

Kathryn from Darlington, County Durham chip-butty country, dropped out of school at Easter 1982 when she won a *19* magazine competition. "I saw the competition and entered it. . . I nearly died of a heart attack when I heard that I had won. . ." recalls Kathryn.

The prize was a £350 voucher for 'Miss Selfridge', a fashion spread in *19* and perhaps a cover. Kathryn got the lot and more. She was taken on by Bookings Model Agency in Covent Garden. "I had really, really short hair then, short . . . and spikey," she remembers. Just like all the other model clones.

Since then her crowning glory has

■ *Far left: Venita Marshall: natural, fresh, healthy look. Left: Deborah Hanna: demure, soft, sultry look. Above: Kathryn Hardy: Bardot-esque*

grown into a beautiful, sleek bob that perfectly frames her round face and full sexy lips, flatters her English Rose complexion. Ms. Hardy's a far cry from your pin-thin Twiggy type. A healthy, outdoor girl, athletic in build (she was still at school, playing netball, and getting masses of exercise), she weighs quite an average 9½ stone, stands 5′ 10″ and her vitals are 32-23-35.

During her short career, Kathryn has been Cover-Girl many times over. This cute, pert little face has graced the covers of *Miss London* twice, *Company* once, both *Woman*, and *Woman's Own* and *The London Designer Collections* Magazine. Added to which the lucky young lass has done spreads for *19*, *Over 21*, *Harpers & Queen*, *Vogue Promotions*, Paris *Elle* and French *Cosmopolitan*. Quite a track record for someone just turned sweet 17.

Says her agent, Patti Carling of Bookings: "We knew that she had the potential for what was happening, but she has proved a real find, coping with all the different personalities; she takes it all in her stride . . . she was thrown in at the deep end and coming down from Darlington and having to find her own way around . . ." "Now the world's her oyster – Paris, Milan, New York, they all want her. And the Germans are crying out for her. Apart from all her physical attributes, she has a very good mental attitude to the business," says Patti, praising her protégée.

Says photographer, Victor Yuan who took Kathryn's pictures for this book: "She is a total blend of innocent naïveté, she can look babyish or raunchy. That little, innocent, sexy look – she exudes it, though she's not fully aware yet of her potential as a woman."

Now to our brunette, Irish-colleen, DEBORAH HANNA. "I love Deborah Hanna's look – she's certainly got that look of the moment, that mouth, those eyes," says Mary-Ann Edgar. Whilst Jo Fonseca, her agent sighs: "I'd like to discover 10 Deborahs every 6 months."

Deborah, 20, hails from just outside Belfast, and came to London in February. "I saw a T.V. programme on Models One, wrote in to them," she said. "She sent us a picture and I sent back a note saying 'Please come and see us otherwise you'll never do it. The day she came, I sent her down to see photographer, Roger Eaton, and she got a *Company* cover." And so another little star was born.

Make-up artist, Mark Hayles says of her: "I think she has a great look, very beautiful, though I also think that she's fortunate to be so photogenic . . . she doesn't look as good in the flesh. The camera's obviously kind to her and that's what it's all about."

But you don't have to be a babe in the modelling wood to succeed. Our redhead, VENITA MARSHALL, from Croydon is an ex-secretary who came to her present agency Select through photographic advice. "They made my image more natural," she says. "I started to grow my hair long but clients didn't really like it, so I had it cut short . . . I'm lucky that I look so young," says this 24-year-old who's an old married lady of 5 years standing. Hubby is a meat-trader – Venita was a secretary when they first met. "He doesn't mind now when jobs go on late, because he can relate to my work in magazines," says Venita. "It's nice for me as most of the people he works with don't know anything about my world – he gets quite a kick out of telling people his wife's a model," muses Venita. And you may have seen her in the ads for Dr. Pepper, Wranglers and Nice 'n Easy. A natural beauty, Venita's wearing minimal make-up, epitomising the natural, healthy look. She's living proof of this new reality creeping into the world of glamour.

These three faces belong to girls going places. But if the last 5 years have spawned younger and younger model girls, there are no hard-and-fast rules. Even if they are, there are always exceptions. Like Lancome's latest girl. 31 is an age when most models are thinking of pulling out, if, indeed they haven't done so already. Lancome, the cosmetic people have broken all the rules with their current choice of 31-year-old ISABELLA ROSSELLINI as their Lancome Girl. In a world that hitherto has been besotted by the cult of youth, this marks a major breakthrough. The man responsible for this original choice is Gilles Weil, Lancome's International Managing Director. The reason for his choice bears out my theory of clothes-horses for courses. "The Lancome Lady is a mature woman, a creature of reality, not a model or clothes-horse. We wanted an independent woman who could make a choice in life. A woman of the Eighties with certain, endearing imperfections, a fair degree of charm and intelligence, more European than American, because we are a French house, but we wanted the image to be as international as possible," he told me. "Isabella came closer to our own concept of The Lancome Girl than anyone else. We saw her pictures in *Elle* and realised that she had other qualities – she was very contemporary, had that short haircut of the moment, was very confident or rather 'bien dans sa peau' as we call it. We realised that she came very close to what we had

■ *Annabel Schofield: most professional*

■ *Left: Isabella Rossellini: totally international Lancôme girl. Above: Debbie Brett: deserves a brilliant career. Right: Vanessa Angel: a name in New York*

in mind, half-Italian, half-Swedish, living in New York, so totally international. Added to which she was Ingrid Bergman's daughter, which is a plus, though that was not our main concern, initially. She is young, dynamic and a real woman with all the attendant problems; she's a woman in her prime, and an excellent linguist. We have chosen a person not a clothes-horse," enthuses M. Weill. And for 35 days per year, for which she is contracted, La Bella Isabella receives the handsome sum of £200,000 a year.

As a fashion editor, for me the model is the pivotal point of the feature – if she is not up to scratch then there is no point in shooting the pictures. So first get the model and the rest will.take care of itself is my maxim. One is, however, somewhat at the mercy of the model agencies. They propose a face, and it's ours to dispose of. "Have you seen . . ? . . You must see her, she's wonderful . . ." And the photographer gets sold the same story which is how model girls are made. Sadly, street-appeal has its obvious limitations and though I hate to say it, today's girls just aren't versatile enough;

too many have only one look. In the Sixties and Seventies when there were fewer, better known faces and less looks in the fashion spectrum, girls were far more professional and more versatile.

They could do their own hair and make-up, in fact they had to. Today, both hairdresser and make-up artist are essential to the team and the overall look of a girl. One is always asked "Hair and make-up there?" Nor do today's models have the longevity of their predecessors. Its all down to casting for a specific story, whereas years ago a model of the calibre of Jean Shrimpton could be all things to all people. Now there are restrictions. Its an odds-on chance that a girl who is right for the 'Bag-lady' look will not look right in an Yves St. Laurent outfit. Very few girls today have both the face and the figure; in fact the total package is low on the ground these days.

That said, I cannot however conclude this chapter without a few words in praise of four contemporary, chameleonic models who, although they have been working for a few years, are now in their prime. They are true professionals who still rate as faces of the year and are gracing the international glossies. They are: VANESSA ANGEL, from Harrow-on-the-Hill currently working in New York, contracted as the Diet Pepsi Girl, a commercial contract that makes her hundreds of thousands of pounds and the first British model in ages to make the cover of *Vogue;* DEBBIE BRETT, who is also working in New York and sadly missed over here, and ANNABEL SCHOFIELD. These are three of the best most professional girls I have had the pleasure of working with. They are the closest we shall get to the Shrimptons or Twiggies of the Eighties. And they deserve brilliant careers.

And my last word goes to little

SOPHIE WARD. daughter of actor Simon, a girl I discovered two years ago, and sent to Models One. She has been catapulted upwards, this fledgling who has been transformed into one of the most beautiful young women of our time. Says her agent, Mary Ann Edgar: 'I adore Sophie Ward . . . I love her almost blandness, she can be anything. . .'

In five years' time we may well witness the revival of the model as superstar. Which is where we came in. . .●

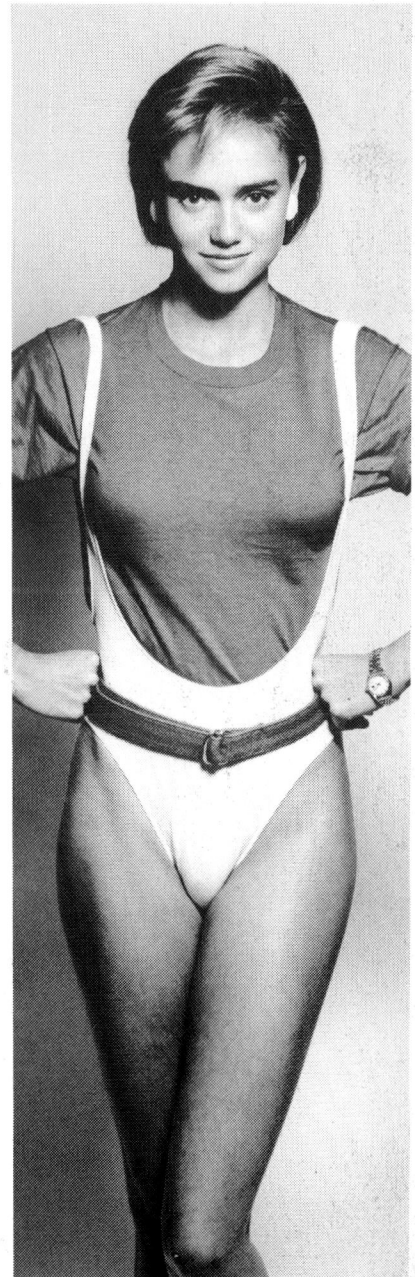

HORRORS

OVER THE TOP

A fashion axiom is that you should never reject any new style as too bizarre or too outré to catch on. What looks hideous at first sight may look just the thing a few days or weeks later when you have "got your eye in", fashion-world jargon for becoming reconciled to the new proportions to the extent of beginning to find them aesthetically pleasing rather than discordantly hard on the eye.

The fashion commentator who rushes into print with paragraphs of outraged condemnation is, therefore, hasty if not downright foolhardy. But some styles remain bizarre however hard the open-minded reporter squints her eye, sucks in her breath and bestows the benefit of the doubt. Because some styles just are bizarre, disfiguring and plain ugly.

However, if the man or woman who designed it has a name which buyers of fashion have learned to trust, the buyer mistrusts her own judgment not the designer's. These people have been identified (by *Women's Wear Daily*) as "fashion victims". Fashion victims are to be pitied, not vilified for they are at the mercy of a system where, all too often, fashion journalists, instead of operating as critics, are either intimidated, bribed or merely flattered into colluding with the designers at the expense of the reader/customer.

Even the most honest of creative artists can give us bad, phoney or boring theatre, novels, paintings and buildings. No less do they give us bad, phoney and boring clothes. But in no other area of artistic endeavour is the artist treated with quite such awe nor does he expect to be. But in the idolatrous world of fashion, a goodly number of designers and, more to the point, designer's managers, partners, PRs and invitation-senders, believe their own overweening publicity. And heretics get banned from fashion shows, refused interviews and denied the friendship of the great.

Here then, is pictorial proof that we ain't scared. ●

■ *If you gum your giant kiss-curl to your eyelashes you will look seductive . . . well you would if it didn't make your eyes water and you didn't keep falling over things you can't see . . . by Ungaro*

■ *Right: A bad fairy struggling to escape her nightmare – dressed by Maryll Lanvin*

■ Jean-Claude de Luca's neat little Ascot number; that's my train you're standing on

■ Chanel's tribute to Carmen Miranda. ■ Right: I got up in a bit of a hurry this morning and lost my lenses down the shower outlet – by Chantal Thomass

■ *The String Vest That Gruesome by Helyett*

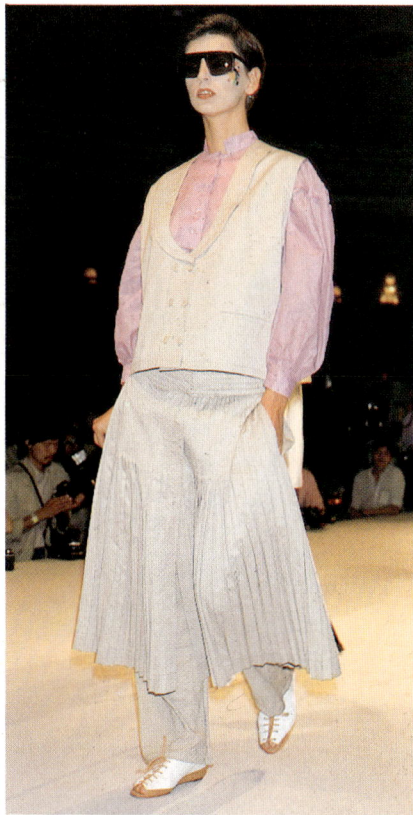

■ *The lugubrious droop, a new look by Claudio La Viola*

■ *Ferreti's glittery little girl's dress on a grown-up*

■ *Bernard Perris's winged pantomime dame's big frock*

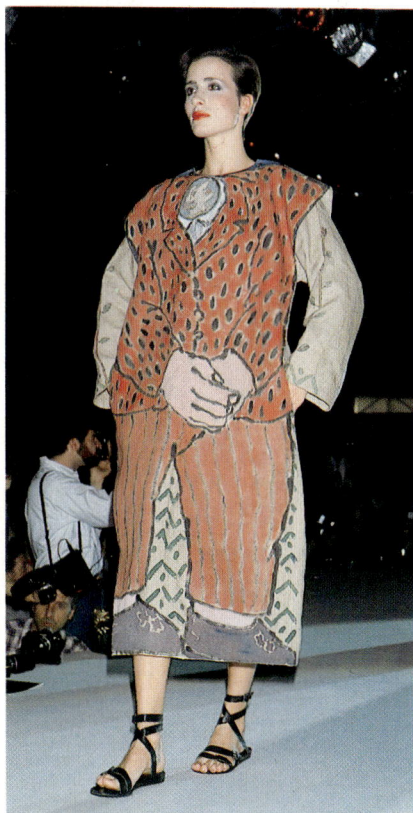

■ *A handy little frock by Jean Charles de Castelbajac*

■ *Vulgar? not at Lancetti's prices. . .*

■ Ungaro's Christmas cracker or who needs to sit down anyway?

■ Militaristic flasher out on the town by Thierry Mugler

■ Broderie anglaise lampshade by Mary McFadden

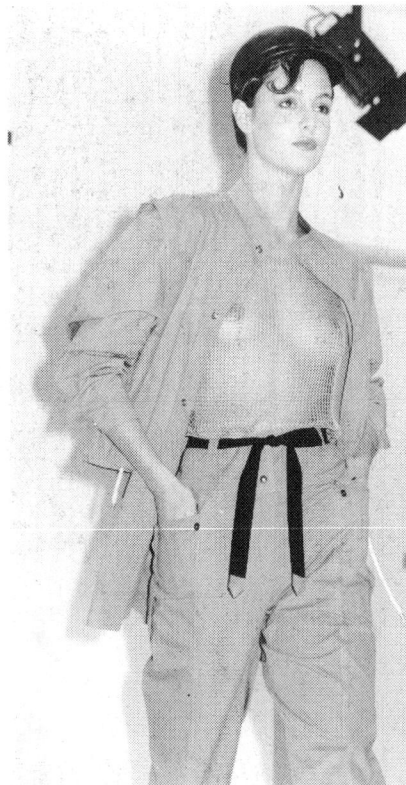

■ It's a boring old trouser suit; let's dye a string vest and show some nipple – Keith Varty for Byblos

■ Gift-wrapped from Amsterdam and blind in one eye by Maryll Lanvin

■ Claude Montana's ambulatory arum lily. ■ Right: Bondage party frock by Fendi

■ *Pearl-studded appliqué doilies on shapeless frock — Geoffrey Beene's home-dressmaker look*

■ *The short-sighted Mexican or how to conceal who it is wearing that dreadful print by Volbracht*

189

■ *Thierry Mugler's plastic chains – can a skirt be an offensive weapon?*

■ *Missoni's sweetie-wrapping*

■ *Well, Karl Lagerfeld was walking down the rue St Denis on his way to his office at Chloé . . .*

■ *All the nice girls love a sailor's jacket, especially by Thierry Mugler with a hint of perversity*

■ *Discreet lace trim by Oscar de la Renta.* ■ *Right: Junko Koshino's absent-minded ballerina*

THE WRITERS

● SALLY BRAMPTON. a former writer on British Vogue magazine, is Fashion Editor of the Observer.

● SHERIDAN MCCOID. former Fashion Assistant on Honey magazine and the London Evening Standard, is Fashion Assistant on the Guardian.

● SUZY MENKES. former Fashion Editor of the London Evening Standard and Women's Page Editor of the Daily Express, is Fashion Editor of The Times and London correspondent of Gap magazine.

● JACKIE MODLINGER. former Fashion Editor of the Guardian, is Fashion Editor of the Daily Express.

● JACKIE MOORE is London Fashion Editor of the Glasgow Herald, woman's page editor of the Countryside group of magazines, Fashion Editor of the Dorchester Magazine and a contributor to the Birmingham Post, the Yorkshire Post and Ambassador Magazine.

● BERNADINE MORRIS. former Fashion Features Editor of Womens Wear Daily and co-author of American Fashion and the Fashion Makers, is Fashion Editor of the New York Times.

● GERALDINE RANSON, former Home Editor of Ideal Home, is Fashion Editor of the Sunday Telegraph.

● SERENA SINCLAIR is Fashion Editor of the Daily Telegraph.

● MARINA STURDZA is a fashion columnist and contributor to the Toronto Star, the Ottawa Citizen, the Edmonton Journal, the Vancouver Sun, Harpers Bazaar France, the Los Angeles Herald Examiner and the Miami Herald.

● THE EDITOR : BRENDA POLAN
After taking a degree in English Language and Literature and the History of Art at Manchester University, Brenda Polan joined the Middlesex Advertiser (Westminster Press Group) as a trainee journalist. On completing her training she moved to Woman's Own magazine as a sub-editor, and then, two years later to Woman, first as deputy chief sub-editor and then as assistant features editor. In 1977 she moved to the features department of the Guardian, becoming its fashion editor in January 1979. She also edits the paper's consumer page and contributes general features to other parts of the paper.

JAEGER

JAEGER

JAEGER

You can tell at a glance.

MOST SHOPS WANT TO SELL YOU MORE CLOTHES.

WARDROBE WANTS TO SELL YOU LESS.

Now that you've read and enjoyed this book we at Wardrobe will give you the guidance to put it all into practice.

Classic designer fashion doesn't change every season, and you need only add slowly and gradually to your wardrobe.

It doesn't have to be extensive, but it must be specifically suited to you and your lifestyle.

We are taught by top European fashion designers and we pass it on to our customers.

We at Wardrobe believe in the Continental idea of buying fewer but better quality clothes.

We also believe every woman is beautiful, but sometimes it takes an expert to bring out her beauty potential.

In the last ten years Wardrobe has dressed Lawyers, Doctors, Actresses, Housewives and Business Women – WOMEN who can't afford to make mistakes.

We try to find clothes that make a woman not only look her best, but make her feel she looks her best.

WARDROBE

3 Grosvenor Street, W1.
(Corner of Bond Street)

17 Chiltern Street, W1.
(Between Baker St. and Marylebone High St.)

The first book on the group that is reviving fashion and elegance in the world of music.

Kid Creole opens his private diaries to music journalist Vivien Goldman in this revealing book from the publishers of **The Fashion Year**

£3.95 Fully illustrated with over 100 colour and black and white photographs

If you cannot find this title in your bookshop, it can be obtained directly from Zomba Books, Zomba House, 165-167 Willesden High Road, London NW10.
Please send cheque or postal order plus £0.60p (paperback) for postage and packing.
Delivery within two weeks.

THE FASHION YEAR IS AN IDEAL
INCENTIVE FOR STAFF AND
CUSTOMERS. FOR TRADE TERMS
ON BULK ORDERS CONTACT:
MARKETING MANAGER,
ZOMBA BOOKS, ZOMBA HOUSE,
165 WILLESDEN HIGH RD.,
LONDON NW10 2SG.

ZB